family circle®

Making beautiful
CAKES

The Family Circle® Promise of Success

Welcome to the world of Confident Cooking,
created for you in the Australian **Family Circle®
Test Kitchen,** where recipes are double-tested
by our team of home economists to achieve a
high standard of success—and delicious
results every time.

MURDOCH BOOKS®
Sydney • London • Vancouver • New York

Contents

Making beautiful cakes 4

Basic recipes

Butter cake 10

Chocolate cake 11

Carrot cake 12

Fruit cake 13

Chocolate mud cake 14

Coconut cake 15

Genoise sponge 16

Classic sponge 17

Spotted collar cake 19

Pink lazy daisy 20

Ice cream fruit box 23

Gateau tiramisu 24

Passionfruit and lemon curd
      sponge 27

Triple truffle cake 28

Christening cake 31

Candied citrus cake 32

Individual Christmas cakes 35

Sugared roses 36

Toffee hazelnut cake 39

Chocolate waves 40

Glacé-topped fruit cake 43

Continental wedding cake 44

Cherry millefeuille 47

Striped chocolate curls 48

Two-tiered cornelli cake 51

Rose petal cake 52

Cappuccino truffle cake 55

Stencil cake 56

Pears with a spun toffee halo 59

Christmas frosted fruits 60

Traditional wedding cake 63

Oranges and lemons syrup cake 64

Chocolate leaf cake 67

Boxes of gifts 68

Toffee circles 71

Star of the show 72

Berry cake 75

Peach and orange mousse cake 76

Floodwork flowers 79

Saint Valentine's day 80

Raspberry tuiles cake 83

Marble glazed cake 84

Striped cake with mango 87

Gold leaf cake 88

Christmas cake 91

Sweet fig and chocolate cake 92

Wrapped presents 95

Wedding flowers 96

Cappuccino ice cream cake 99

Lemon curd meringue cake 100

Strawberries 'n' cream sponge with spun toffee 103

Coconut custard cake 104

Daisy cake 107

Custard meringue gateau 108

Helpful measures 110

Index 112

You will find the following cookery ratings on the recipes in this book:

A single Cooking with Confidence symbol indicates a recipe that is simple and generally straightforward to make—perfect for beginners.

Two symbols indicate the need for just a little more care and a little more time.

Three symbols indicate special cakes that need more investment in time, care and patience—but the results are worth it.

IMPORTANT Those who might be at risk from the effects of salmonella food poisoning (the elderly, pregnant women, young children and those suffering from immune deficiency diseases) should consult their GP with any concerns about eating raw or lightly cooked eggs.

Making beautiful cakes *can seem a daunting prospect when you look at the fabulous creations in this book. But in reality, baking and decorating cakes is easy—simply follow the straightforward instructions below and take time to organize each stage thoroughly.*

HOW TO USE THIS BOOK

Following this introduction you will find the recipes for the eight basic cakes used within this book: a butter cake, chocolate cake, carrot cake, fruit cake, mud cake, coconut cake, Genoise sponge and classic sponge. The basic recipes will give you full instructions on how to make these cakes, with variations of different sizes, shapes and their relevant cooking times in a box after the recipe.

Following the basic recipes, you will find the instructions for making the beautiful decorated cakes. You will find each ingredient list starts by stating what size cake you require and which basic cake we used when preparing the recipe (we will usually give you one or two alternative cakes as well so you can choose your favourite—there are many recipes where several of the basic recipes could be used). So, simply make the basic cake of your choice (you can probably make this in advance—check the storage instructions in the basic recipe) and then start decorating.

How many to serve?

We haven't put serving quantities on our cake recipes because these can be so subjective. Obviously, the richer the cake, the smaller the slice that will be wanted. But as a rough guide, a basic 23 cm (9 inch) cake will serve around 10 people. Our Christening cake serves roughly 20–30 people; the traditional wedding cake serves 70–80 people and the Continental wedding cake about 50 people. If you need to

serve more people, bake some extra plain cakes and ice simply, then keep them behind the scenes and cut and hand out slices with the 'real' cake. Your guests will not suspect that this is not part of your fantastically decorated creation.

CAKE TINS

Cake tins are available in a wide variety of shapes and sizes, from the standard round and square tins to hearts, daisies, diamonds, bells and many more. The standard shaped tins are usually made of aluminium, while the unusual shapes or moulded designs are often hand-made from tin, specially treated to make it food safe. In this book we have tried to use readily available sizes and shapes of tins. You will probably find it useful to hunt out a speciality cake-decorating shop, where you will find a range of tins and equipment that will make your

job much easier. Some kitchenware shops and large department stores also have a good range.

The golden rule to remember with cake tins is to measure them across the base. If you want to adapt a recipe to make a larger cake than the tin size stated, this is possible. First of all you will need to find out how many quantities of the basic recipe mixture you will need to fill your larger tin. So, if the basic recipe is for a 20 cm (8 inch) round cake, take a tin this size and fill it with water. Then pour the water into your larger tin, and keep doing this until your larger tin is full. In this way you will probably find you need two or three quantities of the basic mixture to fill it.

Lining the tin

Average-sized cakes generally only need the tin base to be lined, after a light greasing with either melted butter or oil (don't use a strong-flavoured oil), or a light coat of vegetable oil spray. This is because they don't have a particularly long cooking time. Simply place the tin on top of a piece of baking paper, draw around it and cut out the shape to fit the base of the tin. Other cakes, such as our fruit cake, which are cooked for a much longer time or those with a high sugar content, require extra protection, both around the side and under the base. This is why we specify in the basic recipe to wrap a wad of newspaper around the outside of the tin, and to sit the tin on a wad of newspaper in the oven. Because the oven temperature is low, this is quite safe. When lining the tins, use good-quality baking paper, free of any wrinkles that could spoil your cake's smooth finish.

Making a collar

Some of the cakes in this book are cooked with a collar. This extends the height of the cake, giving a more dramatic result—the basic fruit and mud cakes are cooked with collars to give extra height and protection during cooking. The basic carrot cake also requires a collar if you are using a 20 cm (8 inch) tin rather than a 22 cm (9 inch) one. This is because you are putting the mixture into a smaller space and it would overflow out of the top of the tin.

As a general rule a single layer of baking paper is enough for a collar on an average-sized cake. Larger cakes and fruit cakes will need a double layer of baking paper to make the collar and line the base.

To make a collar, lightly grease the cake tin. Cut a strip of paper long enough to fit around the outside of the tin and tall enough to

Fold down a cuff in one edge of the collar and then make diagonal cuts at intervals up to the fold line.

Place the collar around the edge of the tin, pressing the cuts onto the base of the tin.

extend 5 cm (2 inches) above the top of the tin. Fold down one cuff, about 2 cm (1 inch) deep, along the length of the strip. Make diagonal cuts up to the fold line about 1 cm ($^1/_2$ inch) apart. Fit the collar around the inside edge of the tin, with the cuts in the base of the tin, pressing them out at right angles so they sit flat around the bottom edge of the tin. Cut a circle of baking paper using the tin as a guide. Place the circle of paper in the base of the tin, over the cuts in the collar.

BAKING THE BASIC CAKES

Organization and commonsense are the keys to creating really beautiful cakes. Make sure you've read through the whole recipe before you start, checking you have the right equipment and enough time (often during decorating you will have to leave things to dry or set, sometimes overnight). Line all your tins before you start and preheat the oven. Always have the shelves in the correct positions to take the tins before you turn on the oven—and make sure they will fit in the oven, or you may have to cook in batches.

When making sponges, ensure the eggs and sugar are beaten until the mixture is very thick and will support a figure of eight drawn across the surface. When you are beating sugar and butter together the recipe will state 'until light and creamy'—take the time to do this as it will help your cake to rise.

Making two or more cakes

For many of the cakes in this book you will need to bake two or more basic cakes before you start. Often you will be using two, or even three, quantities of basic mixture. If making three quantities of mixture or more it is best to make a double quantity and a single quantity and gently fold them together before dividing into the tins. The result is

much more accurate than simply trebling all the quantities. We have tried to be as precise as possible with our quantities, but when making two or more quantities of a mixture you may find you have a little left over when you transfer it to the tin. If you don't want to waste this, cook it in a small cake tin or even in muffin tins.

In the oven

Once you have transferred the mixture to the tin, smooth the surface and make sure the mixture has filled the tin completely into the corners. Bake cakes with the top of the cake in the centre of the oven for even cooking and browning. If the top of the cake seems to be overbrowning, cover it loosely with baking paper or brown paper. Don't be tempted to seal the edges or the cake will steam and become soggy.

After the recommended cooking time, the cake should have shrunk slightly away from the side of the tin and be firm to touch, without a wobbly centre. A skewer inserted into the centre of the cake should come out clean—if not, return the cake to the oven until it is cooked through. Fruit cakes can be a little more difficult: do not confuse sticky fruit with uncooked cake. Also, be careful that you don't test the cake through a crack, as this will give a false 'cooked' result.

In our cooking times we have allowed an extra 5–10 minutes for each cake as ovens vary slightly. So cakes can be tested 5 minutes before the full cooking time and may be ready. Some ovens brown unevenly, so it may be necessary to rotate the cake towards the end of the cooking time.

If you are making two or more cakes in different sized tins, don't forget to adjust the cooking times according to the table following the basic recipe.

Sometimes you will be baking two cakes at the same time. If possible bake them on the same shelf, without the tins touching. If your oven isn't large enough, cook them on separate shelves, rotating them towards the end of the cooking time, taking note of individual cooking times (the smaller will take less time to cook). Don't open the oven before the shorter cooking time has expired.

ICING THE CAKE

Before you ice your cake, you want to make it as perfectly shaped as possible, both for ease of icing and appearances. Use a sharp serrated knife to trim the domed top from the cake. For a really smooth surface with sharp corners, turn the cake upside down and use the smooth base as the top of the cake.

Use a sharp knife to cut away the domed top from the cake and give a flat surface.

Cakes that are to be covered with either almond icing or soft icing need to be as smooth as possible, especially fruit cakes. Before you start, plug any holes or gaps in the cake with small pieces of icing.

Before you start, plug any holes in the cake with small pieces of icing.

ALMOND ICING (MARZIPAN see note)

750 g (1¹/2 lb) pure icing sugar
200 g (6¹/2 oz) ground almonds
2 egg yolks
2 tablespoons sweet sherry
2 teaspoons glycerine
1 tablespoon lemon juice
few drops almond essence

Sift the icing sugar into a large bowl, then remove a cupful for use when kneading. Stir the almonds into the icing sugar in the bowl and make a well in the centre. Mix the egg yolks, sherry, glycerine, lemon juice and almond essence and pour into the well. Stir with a knife until stiff.

Use the reserved icing sugar to dust a work surface and knead the icing for 3–5 minutes, adding more icing sugar as necessary to prevent sticking. Knead until the icing is smooth and pliable.

Either use immediately or wrap in plastic and store in an airtight container in a cool place (not refrigerated) for up to 3 days. Makes 1 kg (2 lb).

Note: Almond icing is interchangeable with marzipan, although in Australia pure marzipan can be much more expensive than 'almond icing'.

Both almond icing and soft icing (known as ready-roll fondant in the UK) can be bought in packets or made from the recipes on these pages. Bear in mind that the home-made almond icing contains raw egg yolk, so can't be kept as long as packet icing. It also has a slightly grainier texture than packet icing.

Brush the cake lightly with sieved apricot jam to make the icing stick to the cake. Roll out the icing, on a surface dusted with icing sugar, large enough to fit the cake. Roll onto the rolling pin, then onto the

Roll the icing onto the pin, then unroll it again over the cake.

cake. Dust your hands with pure icing sugar and smooth the icing onto the cake, easing it over the corners and sides. Trim away any excess icing. Pierce any air bubbles with a pin and smooth over the icing with the palm of your hand or a 'smoother' available from cake decorating shops. You can make your own smoother with a smooth-edged piece of laminex and a small wooden block glued to the back.

If you are using more than one layer of icing (often cakes are

If you enjoy making and decorating cakes it is worth investing in an icing smoother.

SOFT ICING

5 teaspoons gelatine
125 ml (4 fl oz) liquid glucose
1 tablespoon glycerine
1 kg (2 lb) pure icing sugar

Put the gelatine in a small pan with 3 tablespoons water. Add the glucose and stir over gentle heat until the gelatine has dissolved. Remove from the heat and stir in the glycerine. Leave to cool for 1 minute.

Sift the icing sugar into a large bowl, then remove a cupful for use when kneading. Make a well in the centre of the icing sugar in the bowl and pour in the gelatine mixture. Combine with a wooden spoon, then use a dry hand to knead until the icing has a dough-like texture, adding a little of the reserved icing sugar if necessary. Turn out onto a work surface dusted with icing sugar and knead until smooth and pliable, adding more of the reserved icing sugar as necessary to prevent sticking.

Either use immediately or wrap in plastic and store in an airtight container in a cool place (not refrigerated) for up to 3 days. Makes 1 kg (2 lb).

decorated with almond icing, then a layer of soft icing on top), leave the first layer to dry for about 24 hours before applying the next. Brush the dried icing lightly with a little lightly beaten egg white to make the next layer stick, then roll out the icing and cover the cake as before. Leave to dry for about 48 hours.

Always keep icings covered with plastic wrap until you are ready to

Use lightly beaten egg white to stick the top layer of icing to the underneath layer.

use, to prevent them drying out and forming a crust. If you are colouring your icing, use a toothpick to add the food colouring drop by drop. Pastel tones are more appealing than overly bright cakes.

When using a spreadable icing, such as a ganache or buttercream, to avoid crumbs in the icing, apply a thin 'undercoat' to the cake first, then spread the rest over the top.

The icing sugar question

You will notice that some recipes in this book call for icing sugar while others state 'pure icing sugar'. If you are using this book in the UK, simply use what is packaged as 'icing sugar'. However, in Australia, these are two different products. Pure icing sugar is just as it says, pure icing sugar without any additions. Icing sugar mixture has cornflour added to prevent lumps forming in the icing sugar and prevent icings from drying out. Icing sugar mixture is fine when you are merely dusting a cake, but for making almond icing, soft icing,

MODELLING PASTE

375 g (12 oz) pure icing sugar
1 1/2 teaspoons gelatine
2 teaspoons liquid glucose

Sift the icing sugar into a bowl, then remove a cupful for use when kneading. Bring a small pan of water to the boil and then remove from the heat. Sprinkle the gelatine over 2 tablespoons cold water in a small bowl or cup and then place this in the pan and stir until the gelatine has dissolved. Remove the bowl from the pan and stir in the glucose until melted. Leave to cool but not set, then pour into the icing sugar and gradually mix to form a dough-like mixture. Dust a work surface with the reserved icing sugar and knead the modelling paste until smooth and pliable. Wrap well in plastic and store in an airtight container in a cool place for up to 3 days.

modelling paste, royal icing and icings which you want to dry hard, you will need to use pure icing sugar. To test which is which, drop a couple of teaspoons in a glass of water and stir. The cornflour in icing sugar mixture will turn the water cloudy, but if you are using pure icing sugar it will remain clear.

DECORATIONS

Once you have iced your cake you will want to add some decorations. Have a browse around your local cake decorating shop and stock up on a few ideas which will help you achieve great looking cakes. A piping bag is an invaluable tool in the kitchen and paper ones are easy to make yourself, as shown below:

Cut a square of baking paper and fold in half diagonally to make a triangle.

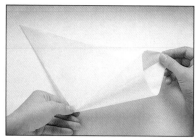

Roll up from one edge to make a cone.

Fold over the top edge several times to secure the bag in position. Fill the bag and snip off the end to pipe the icing.

If you are intending to do a lot of cake decorating you might want to invest in a jaconet piping bag. These have a thin rubber lining so they can be washed (without soap) and reused. They have a screw at one end for attaching nozzles which can be changed any time.

Working with chocolate

You will notice that within this book there is a standard method for melting chocolate—you cannot simply put it in a pan over heat, or it will burn. You need to use indirect heat. Chop the chocolate into small pieces and place in a heatproof bowl. Bring a pan of water to the boil and then remove from the heat. Sit the bowl over the pan, making sure the base of the bowl is not sitting in the water. Stir occasionally, until the chocolate has melted. Take care not to let any water into the chocolate or it will 'sieze' and form a hard mass.

Use indirect heat to melt chocolate. Place it in a bowl over a pan of steaming water.

Alternatively place the chocolate in a microwave-safe bowl and microwave on High in 30 second bursts, testing each time until melted. Microwaved chocolate will hold its shape so don't be deceived—you will need to stir it to check if it has melted or not.

Icing flowers

If you are feeling a little more adventurous, try making your own flowers from modelling paste. Tint a little of the modelling paste with yellow food colouring and roll into balls. Make a hook in the end of a length of covered cake decorating wire and press a yellow ball firmly around the hook to make flower centres. Leave to dry for 24 hours in a dark dry place.

Roll out the white modelling paste on a cornflour dusted work surface and cut out daisy shapes with a cutter. Keep the paste covered as it dries out very fast. Thin out the petals slightly by flattening with your fingers, and form a point on each end. Brush the yellow flower centre with a little water and push the wire through the middle of the white petals. Gently press the petals around the centre to secure.

Stick the wire in a ball of modelling paste covered with plastic wrap and leave to dry. Or lie them on the edge of the table to dry You may have to hang the flowers upside down to dry or the petals will flop back. Remember all flowers aren't perfect. Once dry, store them in an airtight container. Make lots and bunch them together into a posy. Cover the wires with florists tape and arrange on the cake, taking care not to insert the wires directly into the cake (when using wire decorations, make sure you have removed them from the cake before cutting). You can use modelling paste to make a huge variety of figures and flowers.

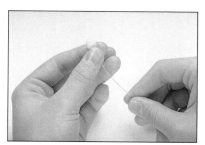

Press the yellow icing ball around the hook on the end of a length of decorating wire.

Use a daisy cutter to cut the petals from plain white modelling paste.

Flatten the petals a little and squeeze the ends into points with your fingers.

Thread the wire through the middle of the petals. Press the petals around the centre.

If you want to paint your icing decorations (rather than tinting the icing before you make them), ensure they are thoroughly dry. Use only a little colour on the brush for a realistic look. Chalks and dusting powders give soft colour and can be dusted straight onto cakes. Scrape the chalk gently with a knife onto a saucer and use a soft dry brush to apply. To tone the colour down, blend in a little cornflour.

CAKE BOARDS

Most cakes can be assembled on plates if you don't own any cake boards. Choose plates that are completely flat across the base so your cake won't dip in the middle. Cake boards can be bought or cut to size from heavy-duty cardboard or thin sheets of wood such as masonite. For heavier cakes use chipboard. Covering your cake board will improve its appearance.

To cover a round cake board, place the board on an upside down piece of paper. Draw around the board, then draw an outline 5 cm (2 inches) larger than the board.

Cut out the paper following the larger outline. Make diagonal cuts to the smaller outline about 1 cm (1/2 inch) apart. Replace the board in the centre of the paper and fold the cut edge over. Stick with tape. Cut another piece of paper slightly smaller than the board and tape or glue over the underside of the board to cover the folded edge.

Make diagonal cuts around the edge of the paper, reaching to the inner outline.

Fold the cut paper over the edge of the cake board and secure with tape.

To cover a square board, cut a square 5 cm (2 inches) larger than the board, then fold in the sides and secure with tape. Fold in the corners neatly as you go.

To secure the cake to the cake board, use a paste made from a little egg white and sifted icing sugar.

Supporting layered cakes

Cakes that are built up in layers, especially heavy fruit cakes, need to be supported with skewers and boards between the layers to prevent sinking. The cakes need to be on boards slightly smaller than themselves. Trace the size of the top cake onto a sheet of paper. Place the paper over the lower cake and use

as a guide to mark where you are going to place the skewers, 3 cm (1 inch) in from the outer edge of the top cake. For square cakes, place a skewer in each corner and for round cakes use three skewers, evenly spaced. Push the skewers point-down into the icing, then reposition point-up. Mark the skewer level with the icing, remove

Mark the skewers level with the icing and cut off at that point.

from the cake and cut off at the mark. Reinsert the skewers (they should now sit level with the icing) and place the smaller cake, on its board, on top. The skewers will now support the weight.

MOVING YOUR CAKE

If you need to transport your cake to a wedding or function, do so with care—after all that work we don't want any accidents. If you are transporting a layered cake it will probably be easier to box the layers separately and assemble when you arrive. Choose a box about the same size as the cakeboard to minimize movement. Cut a strip of thin foam and place it in the bottom of the box. Use a folded strip of baking paper as a 'sling' to lift the cake in and out of the box.

Cakes decorated with soft icing are best stored in a cool dark place in an airtight container, not in the fridge or the icing will go sticky. Add a couple of sticks of chalk, a small container of rice or sachets of silica gel (not letting them touch the cake) in the box to absorb moisture.

Basic cake recipes

out clean when inserted into the centre of the cake.

4 Leave the cake in the tin for at least 5 minutes before turning out onto a wire rack to cool completely.

Storage time: Butter cake can be kept in an airtight container in the fridge for up to a week, or for 3–4 days in an airtight container in a cool dry place. It can be frozen for up to 2 months.

Variations:

• To make a 22 cm (9 inch) round cake, bake for 1 hour 5 minutes.

• To make a 20 cm (8 inch) square cake, bake for 55 minutes.

• To make a 23 cm (9 inch) square cake, bake for 55 minutes.

• To make an 18 x 25 cm (7 x 10 inch) oval cake, bake for 1 hour 10 minutes.

• To make four 9 cm (3^1/$_2$ inch) round cakes, bake for 45 minutes.

• If using a kugelhopf tin, bake for 1 hour 5 minutes.

• If using a 15 x 18 cm (6 x 7 inch) charlotte tin, bake for 1 hour 5 minutes.

Butter cake

Preparation time: 20 minutes
Total cooking time: 1^1/$_4$ hours

280 g (9 oz) butter
225 g (7 oz) caster sugar
1^1/$_2$ teaspoons vanilla essence
4 eggs
225 g (7 oz) self-raising flour
150 g (5 oz) plain flour
185 ml (6 fl oz) milk

1 Preheat the oven to moderate 180°C (350°F/Gas 4). Brush a deep 20 cm (8 inch) round cake tin with melted butter or oil and line the base with baking paper.
2 Beat the butter and sugar with electric beaters until light and creamy. Beat in the vanilla essence. Add the eggs one at a time, beating well after each addition.
3 Using a large metal spoon, fold in the combined sifted flours alternately with the milk, until smooth. Spoon the mixture into the tin and smooth the surface. Bake for 1^1/$_4$ hours, or until a skewer comes

out clean when inserted into the centre. Leave the cake to cool in the tin for at least 5 minutes before turning out onto a wire rack to cool completely.

Storage time: Chocolate cake can be kept in an airtight container in the fridge for up to a week, or for 3 days in a cool dry place. It can also be frozen for up to 2 months.

Variations:

• To make a 22 cm (9 inch) round cake, bake for 1 hour.

• To make a 23 cm (9 inch) square cake, bake for 1 hour.

• To make an 18 x 25 cm (7 x 10 inch) oval cake, bake for 1 hour 25 minutes.

• If using a 15 x 18 cm (6 x 7 inch) charlotte tin, bake for 1 hour 40 minutes.

• To make one 15 cm (6 inch) and one 20 cm (8 inch) round cake, use 2 quantities of mixture and bake for 1 hour 20 minutes and 1¹/₂ hours respectively.

Chocolate cake

Preparation time: 25 minutes
Total cooking time: 1¹/₄ hours

185 g (6 oz) butter
330 g (11 oz) caster sugar
2¹/₂ teaspoons vanilla essence
3 eggs
75 g (2¹/₂ oz) self-raising flour
225 g (7 oz) plain flour
1¹/₂ teaspoons bicarbonate of soda
90 g (3 oz) cocoa powder
280 ml (9 fl oz) buttermilk

1 Preheat the oven to moderate 180°C (350°F/Gas 4). Brush a deep, 20 cm (8 inch) round cake tin with melted butter or oil. Line the base with baking paper.
2 Beat the butter and sugar with electric beaters until light and creamy. Beat in the vanilla essence. Add the eggs, one at a time, beating well after each addition.
3 Using a metal spoon, fold in the combined sifted flours, bicarbonate of soda and cocoa powder alternately with the buttermilk. Stir until just smooth.
4 Spoon the mixture into the tin and smooth the surface. Bake for 1¹/₄ hours, or until a skewer comes

the well, stirring into the dry ingredients until smooth.

4 Stir in the carrot and nuts. Spoon into the tin and smooth the surface. Bake for 1 hour 15 minutes, or until a skewer comes out clean when inserted into the centre. Leave in the tin for at least 15 minutes before turning out onto a wire rack to cool completely.

Storage time: Can be kept in an airtight container in the fridge for up to a week, or for 3 days in an airtight container in a cool dry place. Can also be frozen for up to 2 months.

Variations:

• To make a 20 cm (8 inch) round cake, bake for 1¹/₂ hours.

• To make a 20 cm (8 inch) square cake, bake for 1¹/₄ hours.

• To make an 18 x 25 cm (7 x 10 inch) oval cake, bake for 1¹/₂ hours.

• To make four 9 cm (3¹/₂ inch) round cakes, bake for 1 hour.

• If using a 15 x 18 cm (6 x 7 inch) charlotte tin, bake for 1 hour 40 minutes.

• To make one 15 cm (6 inch) and one 20 cm (8 inch) round cake, use 2 quantities of mixture and bake for 1¹/₂ hours and 1 hour 50 minutes respectively.

Carrot cake

Preparation time: 40 minutes
Total cooking time: 1¹/₄ hours

150 g (5 oz) self-raising flour
150 g (5 oz) plain flour
2 teaspoons ground cinnamon
¹/₂ teaspoon ground cloves
1 teaspoon ground ginger
¹/₂ teaspoon ground nutmeg
1 teaspoon bicarbonate of soda
200 ml (6¹/₂ fl oz) vegetable oil
230 g (7¹/₂ oz) soft brown sugar
4 eggs
125 ml (4 fl oz) golden syrup or
   treacle

500 g (1 lb) grated carrot
60 g (2 oz) chopped pecans or
   walnuts

1 Preheat the oven to warm 160°C (315°F/Gas 2–3). Brush a deep 22 cm (9 inch) round cake tin with melted butter or oil. Line the base with baking paper. If you are making the 20 cm (8 inch) round cake, or using two quantities of mixture to make the 15 cm (6 inch) and 20 cm (8 inch) cakes you will need to put a collar on the tin: see the instructions on page 5.

2 Sift together the flours, spices and bicarbonate of soda in a large bowl. Make a well in the centre.

3 Whisk together the oil, sugar, eggs and syrup. Gradually pour into

Fruit cake

*Preparation time: 30 minutes +
overnight soaking of fruit*
Total cooking time: 3¹/₄ hours

500 g (1 lb) sultanas
375 g (12 oz) raisins, chopped
250 g (8 oz) currants
250 g (8 oz) glacé cherries,
  quartered
250 ml (8 fl oz) brandy or rum,
  plus 1 tablespoon to glaze
250 g (8 oz) butter
230 g (7¹/₂ oz) soft dark brown
  sugar
2 tablespoons apricot jam
2 tablespoons treacle or syrup
1 tablespoon grated lemon or
  orange rind
4 eggs
350 g (11 oz) plain flour
1 teaspoon each of ginger,
  mixed spice and cinnamon

1 Put the fruit in a bowl with the brandy and soak overnight.
2 Preheat the oven to slow 150°C (300°F/Gas 2). Brush a deep 22 cm (9 inch) round cake tin with melted butter or oil. Cut 2 strips of baking paper long enough to fit around the outside of the tin and wide enough to come 5 cm (2 inches) above the top of tin. Fold down a cuff about 2 cm (1 inch) deep along the length of each strip. Make diagonal cuts up to the fold line approximately 1 cm (¹/₂ inch) apart. Fit the strips around the inside of the tin, pressing the cuts so that they sit flat around the bottom edge of the tin. Cut 2 circles of baking paper, using the tin as a guide, and use to line the base. Wrap a folded piece of newspaper around the outside of the tin and tie securely with string.
3 Beat the butter and sugar to just combine. Beat in the jam, treacle and rind. Add the eggs one at a time, beating after each addition.
4 Stir the fruit and the combined sifted flour and spices alternately into the mixture.
5 Spoon into the tin and smooth the surface. Tap the tin on the bench to remove any air bubbles. Dip your hand in water and level the surface. Sit the cake tin on several layers of newspaper in the oven and bake for 3–3¹/₄ hours, or until a skewer comes out clean when inserted into the centre. Brush with the extra tablespoon of brandy. Cover the top of the cake with paper and wrap in a tea towel. Cool completely in the tin.

Storage time: Can be kept, tightly wrapped in plastic wrap, in a cool dry place for up to 8 months or frozen for at least 12 months.

Variations:

● To make a 23 cm (9 inch) square cake, bake for 3 hours.

● To make an 18 x 25 cm (7 x 10 inch) oval cake, bake for 3¹/₂ hours.

● To make one 15 cm (6 inch) and one 30 cm (12 inch) round cake, use 2 quantities of mixture and bake for 2 hours 40 minutes and 3 hours 10 minutes respectively.

● To make one 12 cm (5 inch) and one 25 cm (10 inch) square cake, use 2 quantities of mixture and bake for 2 hours 50 minutes and 3¹/₂ hours respectively.

● To make one 16 cm (6¹/₂ inch) and one 30 cm (12 inch) square cake, use 3 quantities of mixture and bake for 3 hours and 4 hours 40 minutes respectively.

Storage time: Keep in the fridge in an airtight container for up to 3 weeks or in a cool dry place for up to a week. Can be frozen for up to 2 months.

Variations:

- To make a 20 cm (8 inch) round cake, bake for 2 hours.

- To make a 23 cm (9 inch) square cake, bake for $1^1/2$ hours.

- To make a 30 cm (12 inch) square cake, use 2 quantities of mixture and bake for $2^1/2$ hours.

- To make an 18 x 25 cm (7 x 10 inch) oval cake, bake for 2 hours.

- To make one 15 cm (6 inch) and one 20 cm (8 inch) round cake, use 2 quantities of mixture and bake for $1^1/2$–$1^3/4$ hours and 2 hours respectively.

- To make one 15 cm (6 inch) and one 30 cm (12 inch) round cake use 3 quantities of mixture and bake for 2 hours 20 minutes and $3^1/2$ hours respectively.

- To make one 12 cm (5 inch) and one 25 cm (10 inch) square cake, use 2 quantities of mixture and bake for 1 hour and 1 hour 40 minutes respectively.

- To make one 16 cm ($6^1/2$ inch) and one 30 cm (12 inch) square cake, use 3 quantities of mixture and bake for $2^1/2$ hours and 3 hours respectively.

- To make one 18 cm (7 inch) and one 22 cm (9 inch) round cake, use 2 quantities of mixture and bake for $1^3/4$ hours and $2^1/4$ hours respectively.

Chocolate mud cake

Preparation time: 30 minutes
Total cooking time: $1^3/4$ hours

250 g (8 oz) butter
250 g (8 oz) dark chocolate
2 tablespoons instant espresso coffee powder or granules
150 g (5 oz) self-raising flour
150 g (5 oz) plain flour
60 g (2 oz) cocoa powder
$^1/2$ teaspoon bicarbonate of soda
550 g (1lb 2 oz) caster sugar
4 eggs
2 tablespoons oil
125 ml (4 fl oz) buttermilk

1 Preheat the oven to warm 160°C (315°F/Gas 2–3). Brush a deep 22 cm (9 inch) round cake tin with melted butter or oil. Line the base and side with baking paper, making sure the paper around the side extends at least 5 cm (2 inches) above the top edge.

2 Put the butter, chocolate and coffee in a pan with 185 ml (6 oz) hot water. Stir over low heat until smooth. Remove from the heat.

3 Sift the flours, cocoa and bicarbonate of soda into a large bowl. Stir in the sugar and make a well in the centre. Add the combined eggs, oil and buttermilk and, using a large metal spoon, slowly stir to start incorporating the dry ingredients. Gradually stir in the melted chocolate mixture.

4 Pour the mixture into the tin and bake for $1^3/4$ hours. Test the centre with a skewer—the skewer may appear just slightly wet. Remove the cake from the oven unless the centre looks raw. If the cake needs a little longer, give it an extra 5–10 minutes. Leave the cake in the tin until completely cold, then turn out and wrap in plastic wrap.

Coconut cake

Preparation time: 25 minutes
Total cooking time: 1 hour

250 g (8 oz) self-raising flour
45 g (1½ oz) desiccated
   coconut
220 g (7 oz) caster sugar
60 g (2 oz) ground almonds
250 ml (8 fl oz) buttermilk
2 eggs
1 teaspoon vanilla essence
150 g (5 oz) butter, melted

1 Preheat the oven to moderate 180°C (350°F/Gas 4). Brush a deep 20 cm (8 inch) round cake tin with melted butter or oil. Line the base with baking paper.
2 Mix the sifted flour, coconut, sugar and almonds in a large bowl and make a well in the centre.
3 Pour the combined buttermilk, eggs, vanilla and butter into the well and stir with a metal spoon until smooth.
4 Pour the mixture into the tin and smooth the surface. Bake for 1 hour, or until a skewer comes out clean when inserted into the centre of the cake. Leave in the tin for 10 minutes before turning out onto a wire rack to cool.

Storage time: Can be kept in an airtight container in the fridge for up to a week, or for 3 days in an airtight container in a cool dry place. Can also be frozen for up to 2 months.

Variations:

• To make a 22 cm (9 inch) round cake, bake for 55 minutes.

• To make a 20 cm (8 inch) square cake, bake for 45–50 minutes.

• To make a 23 cm (9 inch) square cake, bake for 40 minutes.

• To make an 18 x 25 cm (7 x 10 inch) oval cake, bake for 45 minutes.

• To make four 9 cm (3½ inch) round cakes, bake for 40 minutes.

• If using a kugelhopf tin, bake for 45 minutes.

• If using a 15 x 18 cm (6 x 7 inch) charlotte tin, bake for 1¼ hours (and cover the cake for the last 15 minutes if necessary).

• To make one 15 cm (6 inch) and one 20 cm (8 inch) round cake, use 2 quantities of mixture and bake for 55 minutes and 1 hour 10 minutes respectively.

flour. Using a large metal spoon, fold in quickly and lightly until the mixture is just combined.

4 Spread the mixture evenly into the tins. Bake for 25 minutes, or until the sponge is lightly golden and shrinks slightly from the side of the tin. Leave the cakes in their tins for 5 minutes before turning out onto a wire rack to cool.

Storage time: Can be kept in an airtight container in the fridge or a cool dry place for up to a day.

Variations:

• To make one 18 cm (7 inch) and one 25 cm (10 inch) round cake, use 2 quantities of mixture and bake for 30 minutes.

Genoise sponge

Preparation time: 20 minutes
Total cooking time: 25 minutes

300 g (10 oz) plain flour
8 eggs
220 g (7 oz) caster sugar
100 g (3½ oz) unsalted butter, melted

1 Preheat the oven to moderate 180°C (350 F/Gas 4). Brush 2 deep 22 cm (9 inch) round cake tins with melted butter. Line the bases with baking paper and then grease the paper. Dust the tins lightly with a little extra flour, shaking off the excess. Sift the flour three times onto greaseproof paper.

2 Mix the eggs and sugar in a large heatproof bowl. Place the bowl over a pan of simmering water and beat with electric beaters for 8 minutes, or until the mixture is thick and fluffy and a ribbon of mixture drawn in a figure of eight doesn't sink immediately. Remove from the heat and beat for 3 minutes, or until slightly cooled.

3 Add the cooled butter and sifted

Spread evenly into the tins and bake for 25 minutes, or until the sponge is lightly golden and shrinks slightly from the side of the tin. Leave the sponges in their tins for 5 minutes before turning out onto a wire rack to cool.

Storage time: This sponge is best eaten on the day it is made—it won't keep well as it only contains a very small amount of fat.

Classic sponge

Preparation time: 20 minutes
Total cooking time: 25 minutes

75 g (2¹/₂ oz) plain flour
150 g (5 oz) self-raising flour
6 eggs
220 g (7 oz) caster sugar
2 tablespoons boiling water

1 Preheat the oven to moderate 180°C (350°F/Gas 4). Brush 2 deep 22 cm (9 inch) round cake tins with melted butter and line the bases with baking paper. Dust the tins lightly with a little extra flour, shaking off the excess.
2 Sift the flours three times onto greaseproof paper. Beat the eggs in a large bowl with electric beaters for 7 minutes, or until thick and pale.
3 Gradually add the sugar to the eggs, beating well after each addition. Using a metal spoon, fold in the sifted flour and hot water.

Spotted collar cake

The chocolate collar is what makes this cake so spectacular... once you have perfected the technique, you can use it to make even more elaborately patterned collars for cakes and cheesecakes.

Cut the contact to the same height as the cake and long enough to wrap round it.

one 18 x 25 cm (7 x 10 inch) oval cake (we used mud cake but you could use butter, chocolate, carrot or coconut)

shiny contact
cocoa powder, to dust

Coffee buttercream

2 tablespoons cream
75 g (2¹/₂ oz) white chocolate melts
100 g (3¹/₂ oz) unsalted butter, chopped
40 g (1¹/₄ oz) icing sugar
1 teaspoon instant coffee powder

Collar

30 g (1 oz) white chocolate melts
30 g (1 oz) milk chocolate melts
60 g (2 oz) dark chocolate melts
60 g (2 oz) dark chocolate

1 Cut the dome off the top of the cake to level the surface. Turn the cake upside down on a board so that the flat base becomes the top. Measure the height of the cake. Cut a strip of contact this wide, and long enough to wrap around the cake.
2 To make the coffee buttercream, put the cream and chocolate melts in a small heatproof bowl. Bring a small pan of water to a simmer, remove from the heat and place the bowl over the pan (don't let the bottom of the bowl sit in the water). Stir the chocolate until melted. Beat the butter until light and creamy, then gradually beat in the icing sugar until thick and white. Beat in

the cooled melted chocolate until thick and fluffy. Dissolve the coffee powder in a teaspoon of hot water and beat into the buttercream.
3 Spread the buttercream evenly over the top and side of the cake. In warm weather you could refrigerate the cake for 10–15 minutes after this, to firm the buttercream a little.
4 To make the collar, put the white and milk chocolate melts in separate heatproof bowls and melt as above. Alternatively, melt in the microwave for 1 minute on High, stirring after 30 seconds. Spoon into separate paper piping bags. Pipe large and small dots of chocolate over the shiny side of the contact. Gently tap the contact on the bench to flatten the dots and then leave them to set.
5 Melt the dark chocolate melts and dark chocolate together, then cool slightly. Working quickly, spread evenly over the entire strip of contact, over the top of the dots. Be careful not to press too hard or the dots may lift off the surface. Leave to set a little, but you need to be able to bend the strip without it cracking. Quickly wrap the strip around the cake with the chocolate on the inside. Seal the ends of the contact and leave until set (in the fridge in warm weather). Peel the contact from the collar and dust the cake with cocoa powder.

Ahead of time:

You can decorate the cake and keep it in the fridge for several hours before serving. Don't attempt the chocolate collar on a very hot day—you may find it too soft to work with.

Pipe the melted milk and white chocolate in dots on the shiny side of the contact.

Melt the dark chocolate and spread all over the contact, over the dots.

Wrap the collar around the cake with the chocolate on the inside.

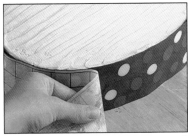

Once the chocolate has set, gently peel away the strip of contact.

Pink lazy daisy

We chose delicate pink daisies and pink feathered icing for our lazy daisy, but you could try simple yellow and white flowers, and tint your icing lemon yellow or pale green.

two 22 cm (9 inch) round cakes (we used carrot, but you could use butter or coconut cakes)

Cream cheese frosting
375 g (13 oz) cream cheese, softened
75 g (2½ oz) butter, softened
90 g (3 oz) icing sugar, sifted
1 teaspoon vanilla essence

Glacé icing
185 g (6 oz) icing sugar
1 teaspoon soft butter
1–2 tablespoons milk or water
pink food colouring

140 g (4½ oz) roasted hazelnuts, roughly chopped
fresh pink daisies

1 To make the cream cheese frosting, beat the cream cheese and butter with electric beaters until smooth and creamy. Gradually beat in the icing sugar and the vanilla and beat until thick and creamy. Set aside ½ cup of the frosting. Slice both cakes in half horizontally and place one half on a serving plate. Spread the cake layer with a layer of frosting and top with another layer of cake. Repeat the layering with the remaining frosting and cake (the top layer of cake will not be spread with frosting). Spread the reserved frosting over the side of the cake and press the hazelnuts firmly all around the side.

2 To make the glacé icing, sift the icing sugar into a bowl, add the butter and enough milk or water to make a thick pourable paste. Tint 2 tablespoons of the icing pink with food colouring and spoon into a paper piping bag. Pour the white icing over the cake and quickly spread to the edges. (Any drips can be trimmed off later when the icing has set.) Pipe even rows of pink icing across the top of the white icing. Before it sets, gently drag a skewer across the pink lines. Then drag the skewer over the pink lines in the other direction—this will give a feathered effect. (The pink icing must be piped over the white icing while they are both wet. If the icing sets there is no alternative but to lift it off the cake and start again.) Leave the icing to set.

3 Trim off any icing that has drizzled down the side of the cake. Trim the stems from the pink daisies and place around the base, saving a couple for the centre.

Ahead of time: The cake can be iced a day in advance and kept in a cool dark place. Don't add the daisies until you are ready to serve or they will wilt.

Pour the icing over and spread quickly to the edge of the cake.

Pipe even rows of pink icing over the top of the white, when still wet.

Drag the skewer over the lines of pink icing, in both directions.

Ice cream fruit box

What a wonderful treat for a summer party. The layer of fruit hides a layer of cake, which in turn hides a secret ice cream centre. Vary the fresh fruit, depending on what's in season.

two 20 cm (8 inch) square cakes
(we used coconut cake, but
you could use butter cake)

2 litres vanilla ice cream
160 g (5½ oz) apricot jam
3 kiwi fruit
1 star fruit
500 g (1 lb) strawberries

Glaze

110 g (3½ oz) apple or fruit
salad baby gel
3 tablespoons sugar
3 tablespoons apricot jam
1 tablespoon Cointreau or Grand
Marnier

1 Remove the ice cream from the freezer and leave to soften a little. Cut the domed tops from the cakes, leaving a flat surface. Keep one of the cake tops (use the other for trifle or cake crumbs). Cut around the inside of each cake but not all the way through, leaving a 1.5 cm ⅝ inch) thick shell around the sides and base. Scoop out the cake from the centre.

2 Fill the hollow centres of the cakes with the ice cream and pack down firmly. Carefully replace one of the cake tops. Wrap the cakes in plastic wrap and place in the freezer overnight, or until the ice cream is completely firm.

3 Warm the jam in a small pan over low heat. Unwrap the cakes and brush a little jam around the edge of the cake that doesn't have a top. Put the other cake on top and press down. Return to the freezer.

4 To make the glaze, put all the ingredients in a small pan and stir over low heat until the sugar has dissolved. Simmer gently for 3–5 minutes, then keep warm.

5 Thinly slice the kiwi and star fruit and half the strawberries (you can peel the fruit, or leave the skin on if you prefer). Place the cake on a board or serving plate and brush all over with the warm jam. Arrange the kiwi fruit and strawberry slices in rows over the top and sides of the cake, pressing them gently so that they stick to the jam. Gently brush the glaze over the fruit. Pile the remaining strawberries on top of the cake and arrange some star fruit slices on top. Serve immediately.

Ahead of time: Fill the cake with ice cream up to 3 days in advance and keep in the freezer. However, once the fruit has been put on the cake it can't be returned to the freezer and so needs to be served immediately.

Remove the centre of the cakes, leaving a shell to be filled with ice cream.

Brush a little jam around the edge of the cake and put the other one on top.

Use the jam to stick the strawberry and kiwi fruit on the cake, in rows.

Gateau tiramisu

Tiramisu means 'pick-me-up' in Italian and that's certainly what this cake will do—rich and creamy, flavoured with Kahlua and coffee syrup, and layered with a mascarpone cream.

two 22 cm (9 inch) genoise
  sponges

1 tablespoon instant coffee
  powder or granules
190 g (6½ oz) caster sugar
80 ml (2¾ fl oz) Kahlua
4 egg yolks
500 g (8 oz) mascarpone cheese
300 ml (10 fl oz) thick cream
cocoa powder, to dust
500 g (8 oz) chocolate cream
  wafers (long thin cigar shapes)
brown ribbon, to decorate

1 Put the coffee powder and 110 g (3½ oz) of the sugar in a small pan with 250 ml (8 fl oz) water. Stir over low heat until the sugar has dissolved. Remove from the heat and leave to cool slightly, then stir in the Kahlua.

2 Beat the egg yolks and the remaining sugar in a heatproof bowl and place the bowl over a pan of barely simmering water. Beat for 3 minutes with electric beaters, or until the mixture is thick and fluffy and leaves a trail on the surface. Remove from the heat and transfer to a cool clean bowl. Beat for 3 minutes, or until cool.

3 Gently stir the mascarpone in a large bowl to soften it. Add the egg yolk mixture, then the cream, beating slightly until thick.

4 Slice both cakes in half horizontally. Place a layer of cake on a serving plate or board and brush generously with the coffee syrup. Spread with about a fifth of the mascarpone cream. Top with another round of cake and continue layering with the syrup, mascarpone cream and cake, finishing with a layer of mascarpone cream. Refrigerate the cake and remaining portion of filling for 1 hour. Dust the top of the cake liberally with cocoa powder and spread the remaining mascarpone cream around the side. Trim the chocolate wafers to stand a little higher than the cake and press gently side-by-side around the cake. Tie the ribbon around the cake and fasten with a large bow.

Ahead of time:
This cake can be stored for a day, covered, in the fridge. Don't decorate with the wafers until ready to serve—they will soften if left to stand.

Beat the egg yolks and sugar in a heat-proof bowl over barely simmering water.

Build up the layers of cake brushed with coffee syrup, and mascarpone cream.

Trim the chocolate wafers to stand just higher than the top of the cake, and arrange them around the edge of the cake.

Passionfruit and lemon curd sponge

The sponge is layered with creamy lemon curd and then drizzled with a passionfuit topping that runs irresistibly down the side of the cake.

two 22 cm (9 inch) classic
  sponge cakes

50 g (1½ oz) white chocolate
  melts

Passionfruit topping
185 g (6 oz) passionfruit pulp
  (you will need 6–8 fresh
  passionfruit)
3 tablespoons orange juice
2 tablespoons caster sugar
1 tablespoon cornflour

Lemon cream
3 egg yolks
75 g (2½ oz) caster sugar
2 teaspoons finely grated
  lemon rind
90 ml (3 fl oz) lemon juice
180 g (6 oz) unsalted butter,
  chopped
300 ml (10 fl oz) thick cream

1 For the passionfruit topping, strain the passionfruit to separate the juice and seeds—you will need 125 ml (4 fl oz) passionfruit juice and 1½ tablespoons of seeds. Put the passionfruit juice, seeds, orange juice and sugar in a small pan. Mix the cornflour with 3 tablespoons water until smooth, then add to the pan. Stir over medium heat until the mixture boils and thickens, then pour into a small bowl, lay a sheet of plastic wrap directly on the surface, and refrigerate until cold.

2 Bring a pan containing a little water to a simmer, then remove from the heat. Place the chocolate melts in a heatproof bowl, then place the bowl over the pan. Don't let the base of the bowl sit in the water. Stir the chocolate over the heat until it has completely melted. Spoon the chocolate into a paper piping bag and pipe lattice patterns onto a sheet of baking paper. Leave to set, then peel away the paper.

3 To make the lemon cream, put the yolks and sugar in a jug and beat well. Strain into a heatproof bowl and add the lemon rind, juice and butter. Place the bowl over a pan of gently simmering water and stir constantly for 20 minutes, or until the mixture thickens enough to coat the back of a wooden spoon. Cool completely (this is lemon curd). Fold the lemon curd into the thick cream and beat until the texture of thick sour cream.

4 Slice each cake in half horizontally. Place one layer of cake onto a serving plate. Spread with a quarter of the lemon cream, then top with another layer of cake. Repeat with the remaining lemon cream and cake, finishing with a layer of lemon cream. Roughen the lemon cream with a fork.

5 Stir the passionfruit topping slightly to make it pourable (thin with a little orange juice if necessary), then pour evenly over the cake, allowing some to run down the side. Stand the chocolate lattices on top.

Ahead of time:
The lemon curd and passionfruit topping can be stored for up to 3 days. Assemble the cake an hour before serving, and don't pour over the topping until ready to serve.

Spoon the melted white chocolate into a piping bag and pipe lattice patterns.

Once the chocolate lattices have set, gently peel away the baking paper.

Stir the lemon curd over the heat until it thickens enough to coat the spoon.

Finish the layers with lemon cream, and roughen the surface with a fork.

Triple truffle cake
There is a simple rule in life...

you can never have too much chocolate. Dark, milk and white chocolates all play

starring roles in this chocaholic's extravaganza.

one 22 cm (9 inch) round cake
  (we used chocolate cake, but
  you could use mud cake)

Chocolate glaze
250 g (8 oz) dark chocolate,
  chopped
125 ml (4 fl oz) cream
165 g (5½ oz) sugar

Truffles
300 g (10 oz) Madeira cake
  crumbs
2 tablespoons jam of your choice
3 tablespoons cream
60 g (2 oz) unsalted butter,
  melted
300 g (10 oz) milk or dark
  chocolate, melted
2 tablespoons rum
150 g (5 oz) each of white, milk
  and dark compound chocolate
egg white
24 carat edible gold leaf

1 Cut the dome off the cake to
give a flat surface. Turn the cake
upside down on a rack over a tray,
to catch the glaze that runs over.
2 To make the glaze, put the
chocolate, cream and sugar in a pan
and stir over low heat until smooth.
Bring to the boil, then reduce the
heat and simmer for 4–5 minutes,
stirring occasionally to prevent the
mixture catching. Remove from the
heat and stir gently, to cool a little.
3 Pour the glaze over the cake,
letting it run evenly down the side.
Tap the tray on the bench to level
the surface. Leave to set completely.
4 Line a tray with baking paper or

foil. To make truffles, mix together
the cake crumbs, jam, cream,
butter, chocolate and rum, stirring
until moistened. Refrigerate for
20–30 minutes, or until firm. Roll
teaspoons of the mixture into balls
and place on the tray. Refrigerate for
10–15 minutes, or until firm.
5 Line 3 trays with baking paper
or foil. Melt the white, milk and
dark chocolate separately: put the
chocolate in a heatproof bowl, bring
a small pan of water to a simmer,
remove from the heat and place the
bowl over the pan (don't let the
bowl touch the water). Stir the
chocolate until melted.
6 Using a fork, dip the truffles in
the different chocolates, tapping
gently on the edge of the bowl to
drain away the excess. Dip a third of
the truffles in the white chocolate, a
third in the milk and the rest in the
dark. Leave on the trays to set.
Don't have the chocolate too hot, or
the truffles may melt and the
chocolate discolour. If you find the
chocolate too thick, add 15 g (½ oz)
Copha (white vegetable shortening).
7 Dab a spot of egg white onto the
dark chocolate truffles, then remove
the gold leaf from the sheet with
tweezers and press onto the egg
white. Put the cake on a serving
plate and pile the truffles on top.

Ahead of time:
The cake can
be glazed up to a day in advance.
Pile with the truffles just prior to
serving (use a little melted chocolate
to stick them to the cake). The
truffles can be kept for 2–3 days in
an airtight container in a cool, dry
place. Refrigerate in warm weather.

*Put the glaze ingredients in a pan and stir
until smooth before bringing to the boil.*

*Pour the glaze over the cake, letting it run
down to completely cover the side.*

*Roll teaspoons of the truffle mixture into
balls and place on the lined tray.*

*Use a fork, or a special chocolate dipper,
to cover the truffles with chocolate.*

*Remove the gold leaf from the sheet with
tweezers and press onto the truffles.*

Christening cake

Commemorate a child's special day with this beautiful cake. Choose pink for a girl, blue for a boy. The cake is iced and the bootees and piped name made several days in advance.

one 18 x 25 cm (7 x 10 inch) oval cake (we used butter cake but you could use chocolate, carrot, fruit, mud or coconut)

21 x 28 cm (8 x 11 inch) oval board
2 tablespoons apricot jam
two 500 g (1 lb) packets soft icing (or follow the recipe on page 7)
assorted food colourings
pure icing sugar
thin ribbon
1 tablespoon egg white
sugar flowers

1 Trim the dome from the cake to give a flat surface. Turn upside down onto the board. Heat the jam in a pan and sieve through a fine strainer. Brush all over the cake.

2 Remove two golf ball-sized pieces of soft icing and one walnut-sized ball and wrap in plastic (for the bootees and leaves). Knead a little colouring into the remaining icing. Roll out large enough to cover the cake, dusting the bench and rolling pin with icing sugar to prevent sticking. Roll the icing over the rolling pin and reroll over the cake. Gently press over the cake with the palms of your hands dusted with icing sugar. Smooth and trim the excess. Leave for a day before decorating.

3 Knead a little green colouring into the walnut-sized ball of icing. Roll out thinly on a bench lightly dusted with icing sugar and cut out leaves with a knife or cutter. Gently press in half, then open out and mark the veins by gently pressing with the back of the knife. Twist at different angles and leave to dry.

4 Knead a little colouring into the golf balls of icing to make it a darker colour than the cake. Roll into two short sausages. Make a bootee by bending the sausage in half and moulding the icing (see step photograph 2). Hollow out the top of the bootee with your finger and thin the edges to make a frill. Leave for 2 hours, then tie a thin ribbon bow around each bootee.

5 Trace the baby's name onto paper in simple letters. Place on a board and cover with non-stick baking paper. Blend the egg white and enough icing sugar to make a smooth icing that holds its shape when drawn across the surface. Tint with colouring if you want. Spoon into a paper piping bag and pipe over the letters. (Pipe a few extra letters in case of breakages.) If the icing is too stiff and doesn't sit flat, while it is still wet, brush gently with a small clean paintbrush dipped in egg white. Leave to dry overnight. Put the remaining icing in a small bowl and cover with plastic. Lift the letters from the paper with a palette knife. Spoon the reserved icing into a small paper piping bag and use a little on the back of each letter, to stick them to the cake. Stick the bootees, flowers and leaves to the cake with icing.

Ahead of time:
Cake can be decorated up to 3 days ahead. If using a fruit cake, it will keep for a month after decorating.

Use leaf cutters or a sharp knife to cut out the leaves, then mark with veins.

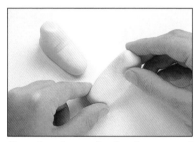

To make a bootee, bend each sausage of icing in half and mould into shape.

Hollow out the top of the bootee with your fingertip, then frill the edge.

Fill a paper piping bag with the icing and pipe over the letters.

Candied citrus cake *The tanginess of candied*

citrus rind appeals to many cake lovers who might find chocolate decorations and

whipped cream a little overpowering.

one cake made in a 2 litre charlotte tin (we used coconut cake, but you could use butter cake)

Candied rind
2 oranges
2 tangelos
2 lemons
2 limes
310 g (10 oz) caster sugar

Lemon icing
125 g (4 oz) icing sugar
20 g (3/4 oz) butter, melted
1–2 tablespoons lemon juice

1 To make the candied rind, use a vegetable peeler to peel the rind from the fruit. Use a sharp knife to remove any pith (the bitter white layer of flesh just inside the rind). Cut the rind into long thin strips.

2 Put the sugar in a pan with 125 ml (4 fl oz) water and stir over low heat until completely dissolved. Bring to the boil, reduce the heat slightly, then add the rind in batches. Simmer each batch for 3–5 minutes, or until the rind is bright and transparent. Remove the rind with tongs and drain on a wire rack until cold.

3 To make the icing, put the icing sugar and butter in a small bowl. Mix in the lemon juice gradually, until the icing is pourable but not runny.

4 Use a serrated knife to cut the dome from the top of the cake to level the surface. Turn the cake upside down on a wire rack and smooth the icing over the top of the cake, allowing it to run down the side, but not completely cover the side. Leave the icing to set. Transfer the cake to a serving plate or stand and pile the candied rind on top of the cake.

Ahead of time: The cake can be kept, refrigerated, for 2 days after decorating. The candied rind can be stored for up to 3 days in an airtight container. Place in a single layer between sheets of baking paper. Refrigerate in hot weather.

Cut away the pith from the rind or it will leave a bitter taste.

Simmer the rind in the syrup until it is bright and transparent.

Turn the cake upside down on a wire rack and smooth the icing over the top.

Individual Christmas cakes *What*

wonderful Christmas gifts these make. They can be kept for up to a month after

icing, so pack them up in tiny decorated boxes and hand them out at Yuletide.

one uncooked fruit cake mixture
   from the recipe on page 13

Holly leaves and berries

60 g (2 oz) almond icing (ready-
   made or see page 6)
green and red food colouring
pure icing sugar

Soft icing-covered cake

100 g (3¹/₂ oz) apricot jam
100 g (3¹/₂ oz) soft icing (ready-
   made or see page 7) per cake
pure icing sugar
thin ribbon

Royal icing-covered cake

1 egg white
250 g (8 oz) pure icing sugar,
   sifted
2–3 teaspoons lemon juice

1 Preheat the oven to slow 150°C (300°F/Gas 2). Lightly grease twelve 1 cup (250 ml/8 fl oz) muffin holes and line the bases with a circle of baking paper. Fill to the top with the cake mixture and smooth the surface. Bake for 1¹/₄ hours, or until a skewer inserted into the centre comes out clean. Cool in the tins before turning out to decorate, so the small base becomes the top.
2 To make the holly leaves, knead 50 g (1³/₄ oz) of the almond icing until it is soft. Roll out on a surface lightly dusted with icing sugar, until 1 mm thick. Cut out the leaves with a cutter or template. Pinch the leaves in half, open out and press

the edges gently to curl in different directions. Dry on baking paper. Brush green colouring around the edge of each leaf—don't put on too much colour or it will bleed.
3 Knead a little red colouring into the remaining almond icing, and roll into small balls to make berries. Paint or roll the berries through the colouring to coat thoroughly. Dry on baking paper.
4 For the soft icing-covered cakes, melt the jam until runny, strain and brush over the cakes. Roll out 100 g (3¹/₂ oz) of the soft icing at a time, on a surface lightly coated with pure icing sugar, until large enough to cover one cake. If there are any holes in the cake, use a little extra icing to plug them and make a smooth surface. Place the icing over the cake and ease over the side, pressing lightly, then trim from around the base. Mix together a little icing sugar and water into a smooth paste. Wrap ribbon around the base of the cake and seal with a little paste. Use the paste to secure two leaves and berries to the top.
5 To make the royal icing covering, lightly beat the egg white with a wooden spoon. Gradually add the icing sugar, beating to a smooth paste. Slowly add the lemon juice until slightly runny. Spread a tablespoon of icing over each cake, using a pallet knife to smooth and letting some drizzle down the sides. Secure holly leaves on top and some berries, using a little leftover icing.

Ahead of time: These can be
stored in a cool dark place for up to a month after icing.

Knead the almond icing until soft, then cut out holly leaves with a cutter or template.

Paint the edges of the tiny leaves with colouring—not too much or it will bleed.

Roll out the soft icing until large enough to cover the cake.

Spread royal icing smoothly over the top, letting it drizzle down the side.

Sugared roses *Roses and cake, what a deliciously romantic combination. Use fresh roses with no blemishes that have not been recently sprayed. The colour is up to you—we chose pink and cream for a hint of spring.*

one 22 cm (9 inch) round cake
  (we used carrot, but you could
  use butter or coconut cake)

White chocolate ganache

150 g (5 oz) white chocolate
  melts
130 g (4½ oz) white chocolate,
  chopped
125 ml (4 fl oz) cream
250 g (8 oz) unsalted butter,
  chopped

2 bunches roses
1 egg white
caster sugar

1 To make the ganache, put all the ingredients in a pan and stir over low heat until melted and smooth. Transfer the mixture to a small bowl, cover the surface with plastic wrap and leave to cool completely. Do not refrigerate. Beat with electric beaters for about 3–5 minutes, or until thick, pale and creamy.
2 Line 2 large trays with paper towel. To sugar the roses, firstly, try to make sure that there is no water between the petals—this will prevent the sugar hardening and may make the roses wet and limp. If you are preparing the roses the day before, leave the stems on and put them back in water even after they have been coated, to help them stay fresh. You will need to pull the petals from one of the roses. Choose some leaves also and set them aside.
3 Place the egg white in a bowl and whisk lightly until just foamy.

Put the caster sugar on a large plate. Take a rose petal and use a small brush to paint the egg white lightly over the petal—make sure the entire petal is coated, but not too heavily. Sprinkle the sugar over the petal, to completely coat, then shake lightly to remove excess sugar and put the petal on the tray. Repeat until you have coated all the petals and leaves.
4 Hold the whole roses carefully and brush gently over and between the petals and down some of the leaves. Sprinkle with the sugar, shaking off the excess, and stand the rose in a jar of water—don't let the sugared area get wet.
5 Leave the sugared roses, petals and leaves for at least an hour to dry, depending on the humidity.
6 Place the cake on a serving plate and spread with the ganache, making swirls with a palette knife. Trim the rose stems and arrange the roses and leaves on top of the cake. Scatter with the petals.

Ahead of time: The cake can be decorated up to 5 hours in advance. In hot weather, decorate just prior to serving. The roses can be sugared the day before.

Note: If you are using carrot cake, you might prefer to use a cream cheese frosting rather than the ganache: beat 375 g (13 oz) cream cheese and 75 g (2½ oz) softened butter with electric beaters until smooth and creamy. Gradually beat in 90 g (3 oz) sifted icing sugar and 1 teaspoon vanilla essence until thick and creamy.

Whisk the egg white until just foamy, then brush lightly over the petals.

Sprinkle the sugar over the petal, then shake to remove the excess.

Brush over and between the petals with egg white, then sprinkle with sugar.

Toffee hazelnut cake *Enjoy the nutty crunch of*

toffee-coated hazelnuts with the smooth chocolate buttercream on this sleek

looking cake—perfect for an occasion where you don't want anything too fussy.

one cake made in a 2 litre
  charlotte tin (we used coconut
  cake, but you could use butter
  or carrot cake)

15–20 whole hazelnuts
220 g (7 oz) caster sugar

Milk chocolate buttercream

2¹⁄₂ tablespoons cream
100 g (3¹⁄₂ oz) milk chocolate
  melts
135 g (4¹⁄₂ oz) unsalted butter
55 g (2 oz) icing sugar

1 Preheat the oven to moderate 180°C (350°F/Gas 4). Bake the hazelnuts on a tray for 5 minutes, or until the skins start to come away. Pour the nuts into a tea towel and rub briskly to remove the skins.

2 To make the toffee, cover a baking tray with foil. Put a heavy-based frying pan over medium heat, gradually sprinkle with some of the sugar and, as it melts, sprinkle with the remaining sugar. Stir to melt any lumps and prevent burning. When the toffee is golden brown, quickly remove from the heat.

3 Use a wooden spoon or two forks to dip the hazelnuts, one at a time, into the toffee. Transfer them to the tray (don't worry if the toffee makes strange shapes) and leave to completely harden.

4 To make the milk chocolate buttercream, put the cream and chocolate in a small heatproof bowl. Bring a small pan of water to a simmer, remove from the heat and place the bowl over the pan (don't let the bottom of the bowl sit in the water). Stir the chocolate over the hot water until melted. Beat the butter until light and creamy, then gradually beat in the sugar until thick and white. Beat in the cooled melted chocolate until the mixture is thick and fluffy.

5 Put the cake on a serving plate or board and spread some of the buttercream evenly and smoothly over the top and side. Put the remaining buttercream in a piping bag fitted with a star nozzle. Pipe large rosettes on top of the cake. Peel the toffeed hazelnuts from the foil and arrange some of them on top of the cake. Serve immediately you've added the hazelnuts. Serve the remaining toffee hazelnuts when you slice the cake.

Ahead of time: The cake can be covered with buttercream and kept in the fridge for up to 2 days— let it return to room temperature before serving. Don't add the toffee hazelnuts until you are ready to serve or the toffee will soften. In humid weather, the toffee will become sticky—if you need to store the toffee hazelnuts, keep them in an airtight container in a cool place.

Roast the hazelnuts, then rub briskly in a tea towel to remove the skins.

Dip the hazelnuts in the toffee, then leave to dry into shapes on the foil-lined tray.

Spread some of the buttercream over the cake, then pipe the remainder in rosettes.

Chocolate waves
For chocolate-lovers everywhere, this spectacular looking cake is really very easy to make. Simply melt the chocolate and drape the shapes over curved objects to create a pile of waves.

one 20 cm (8 inch) round cake
(we used chocolate, but you
could use butter, mud or
coconut cake)

shiny contact
60 g (2 oz) white chocolate
melts
60 g (2 oz) milk chocolate melts
60 g (2 oz) dark chocolate melts

Milk chocolate glaze
250 g (8 oz) milk chocolate,
chopped
125 ml (4 fl oz) cream
2 teaspoons glycerine
2 teaspoons light corn syrup

1 To make the chocolate waves, cut longs strips of shiny contact about 3–4 cm (2 inches) wide. You can make them all the same length or vary them. Melt the white, milk and dark chocolate melts separately: put the melts in a heatproof bowl, bring a small pan of water to a simmer, remove from the heat and place the bowl over the pan (don't let the bottom of the bowl sit in the water). Stir the chocolate over the hot water until melted. Spread a little of the chocolate roughly down each strip of contact (use the shiny side of the contact). Drape the strips over a rolling pin, or different sized bottles to bend them and give interesting shapes. Leave the chocolate to set completely.

2 To make the milk chocolate glaze, put the chocolate, cream, glycerine and corn syrup in a heatproof bowl. Bring a small pan of

water to a simmer, remove from the heat and place the bowl over the pan (don't let the bottom of the bowl sit in the water). Stir over the hot water until the glaze is smooth. Alternatively, melt in the microwave for 30 seconds on High.

3 Using a serrated knife, cut the dome off the top of the cake to level the surface. Turn the cake upside down on a wire rack, so that the flat base of the cake becomes the top. Stand the wire rack over a tray. Pour the chocolate glaze over the top of the cake, then tap the tray on the bench to make the glaze run evenly down the side of the cake. Leave the glaze to set—if the weather's warm you may need to put the cake in the fridge. Scrape the glaze from the tray and gently reheat until smooth (you may need to strain the glaze if there are cake crumbs in it). Pour the glaze over the cake again, tapping the tray to level the surface, and allow to set again. Carefully lift the cake from the wire rack onto a serving plate.

4 When the glaze has completely set, carefully peel the contact from the chocolate waves and pile up on top of the cake.

Ahead of time:
The cake can be glazed up to a day in advance, and the chocolate waves made up to 4 days in advance and stored in an airtight container in a cool dark place. Pile the waves on top of the cake just before serving.

Spread the melted chocolate over the strips of contact.

Drape the chocolate strips over different sized curved objects, to make them curl.

Gently reheat the glaze until smooth, then pour over the top of the cake again.

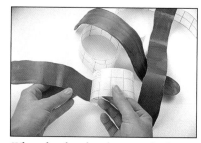

When the chocolate has completely set, peel the backing from the waves.

Glacé-topped fruit cake *This recipe is so*

simple, but will let you dress up a simple rich fruit cake into something special.

We've also included a variation to make twelve individual-sized cakes.

one uncooked fruit cake mixture
from the recipe on page 13

725 g (1¹/₂ lb) mixed glacé fruit,
roughly chopped (try a
mixture of apricots, pineapple,
ginger and cherries)
3 teaspoons gelatine
decorative ribbon

1 Preheat the oven to slow 150°C
(300°F/Gas 2). Line the base and
side of a 18 x 25 cm (7 x 10 inch)
deep oval cake tin with 2 layers of
brown paper and 2 layers of non-
stick baking paper. Wrap 3 layers of
newspaper around the outside of
the tin, securing with string.
2 Spoon the cake mix into the tin
and smooth the surface, using your
hand dipped in water. Tap the tin
on the bench several times to
remove any air pockets from the
mixture. Place in the oven on top of
several layers of newspaper and
bake for 3 hours, then arrange the
glacé fruit over the top. Bake for a
further 30 minutes, then cover
loosely with greased foil or baking
paper to prevent the fruit burning,
and bake for another hour, or until
a skewer comes out clean when
inserted into the centre of the cake.
3 Put 2 tablespoons boiling water
in a bowl and sprinkle with the
gelatine. Leave for 1 minute until
spongy, then stir briskly with a fork
to dissolve. Brush the gelatine over
the hot cake, cover the top with
baking paper and wrap in a tea
towel. Cool completely in the tin,
then turn out and tie with a ribbon.

Ahead of time: This cake is
perfect for making in advance—it
can be stored in an airtight
container for up to a year.

Variation: This recipe can also
be made as small, individual cakes.
Lightly grease twelve 1 cup (250 ml/
8 fl oz) muffin holes with melted
butter or oil and put a round of
baking paper in the bottom of each
hole. Spoon in the cake mixture and
smooth the surface, top with the
glacé fruit and bake for 1¹/₄ hours,
or until a skewer comes out clean.
Then proceed as for the large cake.

*Dip your hand in water and use to smooth
the top of the cake mixture.*

*Bake the cake for 3 hours, then arrange
the glacé fruit on top.*

*Dissolve the gelatine in boiling water and
brush over the glacé fruit.*

Continental wedding cake

For a truly spectacular wedding cake that is a little out of the ordinary, try the

continental variety.

one 18 cm (7 inch) and one
    25 cm (10 inch) genoise
    sponge

White chocolate ganache

150 g (5 oz) white chocolate
    melts
135 g (4^1/2 oz) white chocolate
125 ml (4 fl oz) cream
250 g (8 oz) unsalted butter

Custard filling

75 g (2^1/2 oz) cornflour
60 g (2 oz) custard powder
150 g (5 oz) caster sugar
2 teaspoons vanilla essence
375 ml (12 fl oz) cream
500 ml (16 fl oz) milk
2 egg yolks

185 ml (6 fl oz) Cointreau
300 g (10 oz) white chocolate
    melts, melted
165 g (5^1/2 oz) sugar
cream ribbon

1 To make the ganache, put all the ingredients in a pan and stir over low heat until smooth. Transfer to a bowl, cover with plastic wrap and leave until cold (don't refrigerate). Beat for 3–5 minutes, or until light and fluffy.

2 To make the custard filling, put the cornflour, custard, sugar and vanilla in a pan. Gradually add the cream and milk, whisking until free of lumps. Stir over low heat until coming to the boil. Reduce the heat and simmer for 3 minutes. Remove from the heat and quickly stir in the egg yolks. Transfer to a bowl, cover with plastic wrap and refrigerate for 30 minutes, stirring occasionally.

3 Slice each cake horizontally into three layers. Put the bottom layer of the large cake on a plate. Brush with Cointreau and spread with a third of the custard filling. Top with another layer of cake, Cointreau and custard. Brush the underside of the top layer of cake with Cointreau and place on top. Cover with two thirds of the ganache.

4 Place the bottom layer of the small cake on top of the larger cake. Brush with Cointreau and spread with half the remaining custard. Top with the next layer, brush with Cointreau and spread with the rest of the custard. Brush the underside of the top layer with Cointreau and place on top. Cover with the remaining ganache. Chill.

5 Lay out 2 sheets of plastic wrap. Wrinkle the surface and spread with 2 rows of chocolate about 10 cm (4 inches) high. Leave to set. Break into pieces. Place around the cakes, overlapping the pieces slightly.

6 Cover 3 baking trays with foil. Put a heavy-based pan over medium heat and sprinkle with a little sugar. As the sugar melts, add the rest gradually. Stir to melt any lumps and prevent burning. When golden brown remove from the heat. Drizzle on the trays, cool, then peel away the foil. Tie ribbon around the cake and top with toffee.

Ahead of time:
The cake can be kept for 2 days once assembled but don't add the toffee until you are ready to serve or it will soften.

Slice each of the two cakes horizontally into three layers.

Brush the cake liberally with Cointreau, then spread with custard filling.

Spread the melted chocolate over the wrinkled plastic wrap.

Break the chocolate into pieces, then arrange round the cake, overlapping.

Once the toffee is a dark caramel colour, drizzle over the foil-covered trays.

Cherry millefeuille
A millefeuille is a traditional French pastry—layers of buttery puff pastry are separated by cream and fruit.

We've adapted the idea to use cake, pastry, cherries and creamy filling.

one 23 cm (9 inch) square
  coconut cake

2 sheets ready-rolled puff pastry
six 425 g (14 oz) cans stoneless
  black cherries
40 g (1¼ oz) cornflour
1.25 litres thick cream
125 ml (4 fl oz) Kirsch
icing sugar, to dust

1 Preheat the oven to hot 210°C (415°F/Gas 6–7). Place one sheet of the puff pastry on a tray lined with baking paper and prick all over with a fork (this will be easier if the pastry is slightly thawed). Bake for 10 minutes, or until golden. Repeat with the second sheet of pastry. Leave to cool.

2 Drain the cherries and reserve 500 ml (16 fl oz) of the syrup. Mix a little of the syrup with the cornflour to make a smooth paste. Put the remaining syrup and cherries in a large pan and add the paste. Cook over medium heat, stirring until the mixture boils and thickens. Pour onto a large tray or dish to cool completely, stirring occasionally.

3 Whisk the cream gently until lightly whipped. Use a large serrated knife to slice the cake into 3 layers. Place one sheet of cooked pastry on a board and spread with a third of the cherry mixture; top with one layer of cake, brush the cake with some Kirsch and top with a third of the cream. Repeat these layers twice more and top with the remaining sheet of pastry. Use an electric knife or a large serrated knife to trim the edges of the layered cake so they are even. Transfer carefully to a serving plate or cake board.

4 Dust the top of the cake heavily with icing sugar. Heat a thick metal skewer over a flame until red hot. Hold the end of the skewer with a tea towel and press it over the icing sugar to caramelize the top in a criss-cross pattern—you will need to reheat the skewer several times, wiping off any icing sugar.

Ahead of time: This cake is best made a few hours in advance to give the layers time to settle. Dust with sugar and pattern the top with the skewer close to serving time.

Spread a third of the cherry filling over the first sheet of pastry.

If you have an electric knife, use it to trim the edges of the cake cleanly.

Hold the end of the skewer with a tea towel and drag over the icing sugar.

Striped chocolate curls

The smooth chocolate collar and creamy white chocolate ganache are beautifully topped off by a pile of fairground-striped chocolate curls.

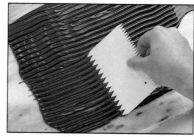

Drag the comb through the chocolate. If you don't have a comb, use a fork.

one 20 cm (8 inch) round cake (we used chocolate, but you could use butter, mud or coconut cake)

White chocolate ganache
150 g (5 oz) white chocolate melts
130 g (4½ oz) white chocolate
125 ml (4 fl oz) cream
250 g (8 oz) unsalted butter

Striped curls
150 g (5 oz) each of dark and white chocolate melts

Chocolate collar
shiny contact
60 g (2 oz) dark chocolate, chopped
60 g (2 oz) dark chocolate melts

1 To make the ganache, put all the ingredients in a pan. Stir over low heat until melted and smooth. Transfer to a small bowl, cover the surface with plastic wrap and cool. Beat for 3–5 minutes, or until thick, pale and creamy.

2 To make the curls, put the dark chocolate melts in a heatproof bowl. Bring a pan containing a little water to a simmer, remove from the heat and place the bowl over the pan (don't let the base of the bowl sit in the water). Stir until the chocolate has melted. Quickly spread fairly thinly over a marble board. Drag a fork or a cake decorating comb through the chocolate. Set at room temperature unless very warm.

3 Melt the white chocolate melts and spread over the dark chocolate. Spread firmly to fill all the gaps. Leave until just set.

4 Using the edge of a sharp knife at a 45° angle, scrape over the top of the chocolate. The strips will curl as they come away—don't press too hard. If the chocolate has set too firmly, the curls will break: leave in a warm place and try again.

5 Cut the domed top off the cake to give a flat surface. Slice the cake horizontally into 3 even layers. Sandwich the layers together with the ganache, leaving enough to spread thinly over the top and side.

6 To make the collar, measure the height of the cake and add 5 mm (¼ inch). Cut a strip of contact this wide and long enough to wrap around the cake with a small overlap. Melt all the chocolate and spread thinly and evenly over the shiny side of the contact. Let it set a little, but you need to be able to bend the the paper without the chocolate cracking. Work quickly: wrap the contact around the cake with the chocolate on the inside. Seal the ends and leave until the chocolate sets completely. Peel away the contact and pile the chocolate curls on top of the cake.

Ahead of time:
The chocolate curls can be stored in an airtight container for up to 4 days. Don't put them on the cake until you are ready to serve. The cake can be iced a day in advance—keep in the fridge in warm weather, but allow to return to room temperature before serving.

Spread the white chocolate firmly, so that it fills in the gaps in the dark chocolate.

Use a sharp knife held at an angle to scrape the curls from the chocolate.

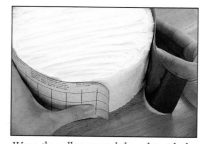

Wrap the collar around the cake with the chocolate on the inside. Leave to set.

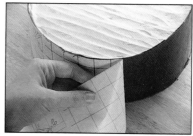

Once set, carefully peel away the contact to leave the chocolate collar.

Two-tiered cornelli cake

This elegant cake is a show-stopper at just about any occasion. We chose cream and purple for a sophisticated colour scheme, but you can tint the icing any colour you like.

two 20 cm (8 inch) and one
   15 cm (6 inch) round cake
   (we used carrot cake, but you
   could use chocolate, mud or
   coconut cake)

Meringue frosting
4 egg whites
220 g (7 oz) caster sugar
330 g (11 oz) unsalted butter

food colouring
round dragees and silver
   cachous
small purple icing flowers

1 To make the meringue frosting, put the egg whites and sugar in a heatproof bowl. Bring a small pan of water to a simmer and place the bowl over the pan (don't let the base of the bowl touch the water). Stir continuously to dissolve the sugar, but be careful not to cook the egg whites.

2 When the sugar has dissolved, remove from the heat and beat the mixture with electric beaters for 5 minutes, or until stiff peaks form. Cut the butter into about 10 pieces and add, piece by piece, beating after each addition. The mixture should thicken when you have about 2 pieces of butter left, but continue until you have added all the butter.

3 Using a sharp serrated knife, trim the domed top from each cake to give a level surface. Place a large cake upside down on a plate, so that the flat base becomes the top. Spread some of the frosting evenly over the top and side of the cake with a palette or flat-bladed knife. Sandwich with the other large cake, then spread frosting over the top and side. Put the small cake on top. Reserve about 3 tablespoons of the frosting and spread the remainder smoothly over the top cake.

4 Add a few drops of food colouring to the reserved frosting to tint it a pale colour (we used purple) and spoon into a small paper icing bag. Pipe squiggles over the top and side of the cake. Use a pair of tweezers to decorate with the dragees, cachous and icing flowers.

Ahead of time:
This cake can be decorated up to 2 days in advance. Keep the two halves separately in airtight containers in the fridge (unless you have an enormous container that will hold the whole cake). Reassemble and allow to return to room temperature before serving.

Beat until stiff peaks form, then beat in the butter, piece by piece.

Place the small cake on top of the other two iced cakes.

Tint the frosting a pale colour and pipe in squiggles over the cake.

Use tweezers to place the dragees, cachous and flowers on the cake.

Rose petal cake

This beautiful and amusing cake brings your garden straight to the tea table. Choose blemish-free roses that haven't been sprayed recently.

one cake made in a 2 litre charlotte tin (we used butter cake, but you could use chocolate or coconut cake)

1 bunch pale pink roses
3 white roses
1 egg white
caster sugar

Meringue frosting
3 egg whites
165 g (5¹/₂ oz) caster sugar
250 g (8 oz) unsalted butter

1 Line 2 or 3 large trays with paper towel. Carefully separate the rose petals, discarding any that are very small or blemished. Whisk the egg white lightly until just foamy. Spread the caster sugar on a large plate. Use a small brush to paint the egg white lightly over the petal—make sure the entire petal is coated, but not too heavily. Sprinkle the petals with caster sugar, gently shake off the excess and put the petals on the tray to dry. Leave them for at least 1 or 2 hours. The drying time may vary according to to the weather and the humidity.
2 To make the meringue frosting, put the egg whites and sugar in a heatproof bowl. Bring a small pan of water to a simmer and place the bowl over the pan (don't let the base of the bowl touch the water). Stir continuously to dissolve the sugar, but be careful not to cook the egg whites.
3 When the sugar has dissolved,

remove the bowl from over the pan and beat the mixture with electric beaters for 3–5 minutes, or until stiff peaks form. Cut the butter into about 10 pieces and add, piece by piece, beating after each addition. The mixture should thicken when you have about 2 pieces of butter left, but continue until you have added all of it.
4 Place the cake on a serving plate. Spread the frosting evenly over the cake, as smoothly as possible. Starting from the base, press a layer of pink rose petals around the cake. Start the next layer slightly overlapping the first and continue working up towards the top of the cake. In the final few layers, alternate white petals with the pink. The cake should look like an open flower from the top.

Ahead of time:
This cake can be decorated up to a day in advance as long as the rose petals are dry. Store in a cool dark place in an airtight container.

Paint egg white over the petals, so they are covered, but not too heavily.

Sprinkle the caster sugar over the petals, then shake off the excess.

Press a layer of petals around the base of the cake then overlap the layers upwards.

Cappuccino truffle cake

This cake is a true indulgence. Once you've learnt how to make your own cappuccino truffles, you might never come out of the kitchen again.

two 23 cm (9 inch) square cakes (we used butter cake, but you could use chocolate or coconut cake)

Coffee buttercream
170 ml (5½ fl oz) cream
300 g (10 oz) white chocolate melts
400 g (13 oz) unsalted butter
160 g (5½ oz) icing sugar
1 tablespoon instant coffee powder

200 g (6½ oz) hazelnuts, roasted and roughly chopped
16 Ferrero Rocher chocolates
cocoa powder, to dust

Cappuccino truffles
80 ml (2¾ fl oz) cream
250 g (8 oz) dark chocolate, finely chopped
3 teaspoons Kahlua
2 teaspoons instant coffee powder
200 g (6½ oz) white chocolate melts

1 To make the coffee buttercream, put the cream and chocolate in a small heatproof bowl. Bring a small pan of water to a simmer, remove from the heat and place the bowl over the pan (don't let the bottom of the bowl sit in the water). Stir over the hot water until melted. Beat the butter until light and creamy, then gradually beat in the sugar until thick and white. Beat in the cooled melted chocolate until thick and fluffy. Dissolve the instant coffee in a tablespoon of hot water, cool, then beat into the buttercream.

2 Put one cake on a serving plate or board. Spread with a quarter of the buttercream and sandwich with the other cake. Cover with the remaining buttercream. Press the hazelnuts onto the side of the cake.

3 To make the truffles, bring the cream to the boil in a small pan, then remove from the heat. Add the dark chocolate and stir until melted. Stir in the Kahlua and coffee. Transfer to a small bowl, cover and refrigerate until cold and thick.

4 Roll rounded teaspoons of the mixture into balls (you should be able to make 25 truffles). Place on a baking tray lined with baking paper and chill until firm. If the mixture is too soft to roll, drop rounded teaspoons of mixture onto the tray and refrigerate for 15 minutes to firm up before rolling into balls.

5 Melt the chocolate melts in a heatproof bowl, cool slightly, then use a spoon and fork to dip and coat the truffles in the chocolate. Place on a clean piece of baking paper and refrigerate for about 15 minutes to set the chocolate.

6 Pile the truffles and chocolates on top of the cake, using any remaining melted chocolate to hold them in place. Dust with cocoa.

Ahead of time
The truffles can be made up to a week in advance and stored in an airtight container in the fridge. The cake can be assembled up to 3 days in advance and kept in an airtight container in the fridge—let it come back to room temperature before serving.

Beat in the cream and melted chocolate until the mixture is thick and fluffy.

Cover the cake with buttercream and stick the hazelnuts to the sides.

Roll rounded teaspoons of the truffle mixture into balls.

Use a fork and a spoon to dip and coat the truffles in melted chocolate.

Stencil cake
This deliciously rich mud cake is one for the budding artists in the kitchen. Making your own stencil is as easy or as difficult as you want it to be—you can let your imagination run wild.

one 23 cm (9 inch) square cake
(we used mud cake, but you
could use chocolate cake)

1 sheet of cardboard for the
stencil
dark cocoa powder, to dust
chocolate sticks, to decorate

Dark chocolate buttercream
90 g (3 oz) dark chocolate,
chopped
150 g (5 oz) unsalted butter
2 tablespoons icing sugar

1 Put the cake on the piece of cardboard and draw around the outside to make an outline. Using a serrated knife, cut the domed top off the cake to leave a flat surface. If you want, trim the sides of the cake to make a very even, sharp-edged square. Turn the cake upside down on a cake board or serving plate, so that the flat base of the cake becomes the top.

2 Draw a design on the cardboard and cut out with a scalpel or sharp scissors. Try to use a firm piece of board so the stencil won't be too floppy.

3 To make the buttercream, bring a pan containing a little water to a simmer. Put the chocolate in a heatproof bowl, remove the pan from the heat and place the bowl over the pan (don't let the base of the bowl sit in the water). Stir the chocolate until melted. Beat the butter with electric beaters until light and creamy. Gradually beat in the cooled melted chocolate and icing sugar and continue beating until pale and creamy. Spread the buttercream evenly over the top and sides of the cake, smoothing the surface as cleanly as possible with a palette knife. Refrigerate for 30 minutes, or until the buttercream is firm.

4 Gently place the stencil over the top of the cake. Place a small amount of cocoa powder in a fine sieve and shake lightly over the stencil. Carefully lift the stencil off the cake without spilling any cocoa that is still on the cardboard. Press the chocolate sticks, upright, around the side of the cake—if they are too long, or uneven, trim them all so they stand just a little higher than the top of the cake.

Ahead of time:
This cake can be decorated up to 2 days in advance. Store in the fridge in warm weather, or in an airtight container in a cool, dry place.

Cut the cardboard to the same size as the cake, draw on a design and cut out.

Spread the buttercream evenly over the top and sides of the cake.

Place the stencil over the top of the cake and shake the cocoa powder over it.

Pears with a spun toffee halo

Choose the smallest pears you can find to make this delightful and whimsical cake,

so they just poke out of the pecan-covered butter cake.

one uncooked butter cake
  mixture from the recipe on
  page 10

1 cinnamon stick
2 strips lemon rind
1 tablespoon lemon juice
440 g (14 oz) caster sugar
6 beurre bosc or packham pears
3 tablespoons apricot jam
2 tablespoons chopped pecans
icing sugar, to dust

1 Put the cinnamon, lemon rind, juice, 1 litre water and half the sugar in a pan large enough to hold the pears and stir over heat until the sugar has dissolved. Core the pears through the bases with a melon baller, then peel and place in the syrup. Simmer, partly covered, for 10 minutes, or until tender. Remove from the heat and leave to cool in the syrup. Drain and leave on paper towel to drain thoroughly.

2 Preheat the oven to moderate 180°C (350°F/Gas 4). Lightly grease two 23 cm (9 inch) round spring-form tins and cover the bases with baking paper. Divide the cake mixture between the tins. Arrange the pears around the edge of one cake, about 2 cm (1 inch) in from the edge, and gently press into the mixture. Bake for 40 minutes, or until a skewer inserted into the centre of the plain cake comes out clean. Cook the pear cake for a further 40 minutes, or until a skewer comes out clean. Leave the cakes in their tins for 5 minutes, before removing.

3 Warm and strain the jam and spread some over the plain cake—if the top is domed, trim it flat. Sit the pear cake on top and brush with a little jam. Sprinkle with the pecans.

4 For the spun toffee, place a couple of sheets of newspaper on the floor where you will be spinning the toffee. Place a wooden spoon on the work surface with its handle over the edge, above the newspaper (weigh it down with a heavy object). Lightly oil the spoon handle. Put a heavy-based pan over medium heat, gradually sprinkle with some of the remaining sugar and, as it melts, sprinkle with the rest. Stir to melt any lumps and prevent burning. Meanwhile, run a little cold water into the sink. When the toffee is golden brown, remove the pan from the heat and place the base in the water to quickly cool the toffee and prevent it burning. This will also make the toffee thicken.

5 Hold two forks back to back and dip in the hot toffee. Carefully flick the toffee backwards and forwards over the handle of the spoon, redipping in the pan as often as necessary—you may need to do this several times. If the toffee gets too thick, warm it slightly over low heat. Lift the toffee off the spoon and mould into a large halo shape, about the same width as the top of the pears. Make a couple more halos and place over the pears.

Ahead of time: Best eaten on the day of baking. The toffee can be kept in an airtight container for several hours, but don't place on the cake until ready to serve.

Core the pears through the base with a melon baller, then peel.

Arrange the poached pears around the edge of the cake mixture in the tin.

As the sugar in the pan melts, sprinkle with more sugar. Stir to melt any lumps.

Flick the toffee backwards and forwards over the handle of the wooden spoon.

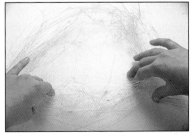

Lift the spun toffee off the spoon and mould into a halo shape.

Christmas frosted fruits *For something a*

little different at Christmas time, sugar coat a collection of berries, currants and

tiny stone fruit and pile them high on this traditional fruit cake.

one 18 x 25 cm (7 x 10 inch)
    oval fruit cake

selection of seasonal fruits such
    as white and dark cherries, red
    or white currants,
    blackcurrants, apricots or
    tiny plums or pears
1 egg white
caster sugar

Icing
1 egg white
1–3 teaspoons lemon juice
125 g (4 oz) pure icing sugar,
    sifted

1 Wash the fruit and make sure it is completely dry before starting (if possible, wash beforehand and leave for several hours). Line a tray with paper towel. Place the egg white in a shallow bowl and whisk until just foamy. Put some caster sugar on a large plate. Work with one piece of fruit at a time, except for the berries which can be sugared in small bunches. Brush the egg white lightly over the fruit, making sure the entire piece of fruit is covered but not too heavily.

2 Sprinkle the sugar over the fruit and shake off any excess, then leave on the tray to dry. The drying time will depend on the humidity. Always frost more fruit than you need, so you have a good selection to choose from when arranging.

3 To make the icing, whisk the egg white until just foamy. Beat in 1 teaspoon of the lemon juice. Add the icing sugar gradually, beating well after each addition. The icing should be thick and white—add a little more lemon juice if necessary, but don't make it too runny.

4 Place the cake on a serving plate or stand. Working quickly, pour the icing over the top. Using a palette knife, carefully smooth the icing to the edge of the cake, allowing it to run slowly down the side. Leave the cake for 10 minutes to let the icing set a little. Arrange the frosted fruits on top of the cake.

Ahead of time: The fruits can be frosted several hours in advance.

Paint the fruit with a little egg white, then sprinkle with the caster sugar.

To make the icing, whisk the egg white, then add lemon juice and icing sugar.

Smooth the icing over the cake, allowing it to run slowly down the side.

Traditional wedding cake *There are*

few more rewarding experiences for a cake-maker than creating a truly beautiful

wedding cake. Celebrate in style with this traditional beauty.

Gently press your finger into the rounded end of the petal and make a hollow.

When all five petals are ready, gently roll them together, pinching the ends.

Put the flower into a padded egg carton, then ease open the petals.

one 30 cm (12 inch) and one
    15 cm (6 inch) round cake (we
    used fruit cake, but you could
    use mud cake)

1 quantity modelling paste (use
    ready-made or see page 7)
cornflour and icing sugar, to
    dust
medium frangipani petal cutter
edible yellow chalks and green,
    brown, yellow food colourings
medium long leaf cutter
15 cm (6 inch) and 40 cm
    (16 inch) round cake boards
2 tablespoons apricot jam
3 x 500 g (1 lb) packets soft
    icing (or use the recipe on
    page 7)
4 wooden skewers
1 teaspoon egg white
1–2 tablespoons pure icing sugar
ribbon

1 Roll a small amount of modelling paste to 2 mm thick on a bench lightly dusted with cornflour and, working quickly, cut out petals with a cutter. Only cut 10 petals at a time (enough for 2 frangipanis) and cover with plastic wrap. Dust your fingers lightly with cornflour and smooth the cut edges of the petal. Gently press your finger into the rounded end of the petal and make a slight hollow by easing your finger towards you. Place a dab of water at the point of each petal and press the next petal, slightly overlapping, onto this. When all five petals are ready, gently roll together, pinching the ends to join. Put in a padded egg carton and ease the petals open to form a full flower. Make at least 20 flowers, all at varying degrees of opening. Make buds by rolling cigar shapes and pressing lines down outside, then give a gentle twist. When dry, dust the centre of the flower with a little yellow chalk.

2 Knead green food colouring into a little modelling paste. Roll out thinly on a bench lightly dusted with cornflour and, with an elongated leaf cutter or sharp knife, cut out leaves about 5 cm (2 inches) long. Gently press in half, then open out and mark veins on either side with the back of the knife. Twist at angles and leave to dry before placing in airtight containers. Paint with green and brown colouring and a little water. Leave to dry.

3 Trim the domes from the cakes so they are the same height. Invert onto the boards. Heat the jam, strain and brush all over the cakes.

4 Knead the icing on a work surface dusted with icing sugar. Add enough yellow colouring to tint cream. Roll two thirds of the icing out to 5 mm (1/4 inch) thick and large enough to cover the large cake. Roll the icing over the rolling pin and reroll over the top of the cake. Press and smooth over the cake, using the palms of your hands dusted with icing sugar. Trim off any excess. Repeat with remaining icing and small cake. Leave the icing to dry for a day before decorating.

5 Insert skewers into the bottom cake, equal distances apart, so they will be covered by the top cake (see page 9). Cut off level with the icing. Place the small cake on top.

6 Mix the egg white into a soft paste with a little icing sugar. Wrap ribbon around the base of each cake and secure with paste; hold with pins while the paste dries (don't forget to remove them before serving the cake). Arrange the flowers and leaves on the cakes, securing with paste.

Ahead of time: Dry the flowers for at least 24 hours. Then they can be kept for 1 month in an airtight container with a stick of chalk or a little raw rice to absorb any moisture. The decorated fruit cake can be kept for up to 1 year, but the mud cake for only 1 week.

Oranges and lemons syrup

cake *This simple cake conjures up the colours and flavours of summer. It*

makes a great finale to an al fresco lunch, served with a dollop of thick cream.

one cake made in a 1.5 litre
capacity kugelhopf tin (we
used coconut cake, but you
could use a butter cake)

2 oranges
2 lemons
up to 500 g (1 lb) caster sugar

1 Cut the oranges and lemons into
thin slices, without peeling them.
Place 250 g (8 oz) of the sugar in a
heavy-based frying pan with 80 ml
(2³/4 fl oz) water. Stir over low heat
until the sugar has completely
dissolved. Bring to the boil, then
reduce the heat to a simmer. Add a
quarter of the sliced fruit to the
syrup and leave to simmer for
5–10 minutes, or until transparent
and toffee-like. Lift out the fruit
with tongs and cool on a wire rack.
2 Add an extra 90 g (3 oz) of
sugar to the syrup and stir gently to
dissolve—the juice from the fruit
breaks down the concentrated syrup
and the fruit won't candy properly
unless you add the sugar. Now you
are ready to simmer the second
batch of sliced fruit. Add 90 g (3 oz)
of sugar to the syrup after cooking
each batch.
3 When all the fruit has been
candied, put the cake on a wire rack
over a tray. Pour the hot syrup over
the cake, allowing it to soak in—if
the syrup is too thick, thin it down
with a little orange juice. Put the
cake on a serving plate. When the
fruit slices have firmed, arrange
them on top of the cake (you can
cut and twist some of the slices).

Ahead of time: The candied
fruit can be kept between layers of
baking paper in an airtight
container for up to 2 days. The cake
should be served within a few hours
of decorating.

Note: You can bake this cake in a
20 cm (8 inch) round tin if you
don't have a kugelhopf tin.

Variation: If blood oranges are
in season, they can look fabulous on
this cake. They must, however, be
treated with extra care as they can
fall apart easily in the sugar syrup.

*Add a quarter of the thinly sliced fruit to
the simmering sugar syrup.*

*Simmer the fruit for 5–10 minutes, or
until transparent and toffee-like.*

*Put the cake on a rack over a tray to
catch the syrup that runs over.*

Chocolate leaf cake *This cake is simple to make*

and also fun, especially if you have children who enjoy helping out in the kitchen.

What better way to spend a rainy afternoon, than painting leaves with chocolate?

one 20 cm (8 inch) round cake (we used mud cake, but you could use chocolate cake)

Dark chocolate glaze
250 g (8 oz) dark chocolate, chopped
125 ml (4 fl oz) cream
2 teaspoons glycerine
2 teaspoons light corn syrup

90 g (3 oz) white chocolate melts
90 g (3 oz) milk chocolate melts
90 g (3 oz) dark chocolate melts
assorted non-toxic leaves

1 To make the dark chocolate glaze, put the chocolate, cream, glycerine and corn syrup in a heatproof bowl. Bring a small pan of water to a simmer, remove from the heat and place the bowl over the pan (don't let the bottom of the bowl sit in the water). Stir over the hot water until the glaze is smooth. Alternatively, melt in the microwave for 30 seconds on High.

2 Using a serrated knife, cut the domed top off the cake to give a flat surface. Turn the cake upside down on a wire rack, so that the flat base becomes the top. Stand the wire rack over a tray, to catch any glaze that may drip. Pour the glaze over the top of the cake and allow it to run evenly down the sides of the cake, completely coating it. Tap the tray on the bench to give a level surface. Put the cake in the refrigerator for 10–15 minutes to let the glaze set.

3 Line 2 oven trays with baking paper. Melt the white, milk and dark chocolate melts separately: put the melts in a heatproof bowl, bring a small pan of water to a simmer, remove from the heat and place the bowl over the pan (don't let the bottom of the bowl sit in the water). Stir the chocolate over the hot water until melted. Alternatively, melt in the microwave for 1 minute on High, stirring after 30 seconds.

4 Make sure your leaves are clean and dry. Using a small brush, brush chocolate over one side of each leaf. Brush some leaves on the smooth side and some on the vein side. On some of the leaves you could use two or three different coloured chocolates. Always coat more leaves than you think you will need, just in case some break. Place the leaves on the lined trays to dry. Spoon a little of the dark chocolate into a small paper icing bag, snip off the end and pipe twigs onto one of the trays. Leave to set.

5 Carefully peel the leaves away from the chocolate. Put the cake on a serving plate or stand and pile the leaves and twigs on top.

Ahead of time: This cake can be decorated up to 2 days in advance and kept refrigerated— but allow it to return to room temperature before serving. The leaves can be stored for up to a week in an airtight container in a cool, dark place.

Note: If you prefer, use milk chocolate instead of dark in the chocolate glaze.

Melt the three chocolates separately and then paint over the leaves.

Spoon some of the dark chocolate into a piping bag to make twigs.

Once the chocolate has set, carefully peel away the leaves.

Boxes of gifts *Spectacular for almost any occasion—*

birthday, wedding or even a christening—this colourful centrepiece will be

welcome at any gathering.

one 12 cm (5 inch) square and
one 25 cm (10 inch) square
fruit cake
one 16 cm (6¹/₂ inch) square
and one 30 cm (12 inch)
square mud cake

80 g (2³/₄ oz) apricot jam
9 x 500 g (8 oz) packets ready-
made soft icing (or see page 7)
pure icing sugar, to dust
assorted food colourings
wooden skewers
1 egg white

1 Cut 3 cardboard squares the same size as the 3 smaller cakes. Trim the tops off the cakes so they are similar heights. Invert the cakes onto the cardboard and a covered cake board. Warm the jam, strain and brush over the cakes.
2 Knead 3¹/₂ packets of the icing on a work surface dusted with icing sugar. Tint the icing pale pink. Roll out the icing to about 5 mm (¹/₄ inch) thick and large enough to cover the largest cake, dusting the bench and rolling pin with icing sugar to prevent sticking. Use a little icing to fill in any holes in the cake, to ensure an even surface. Roll the icing over the rolling pin and reroll over the top of the cake. Gently press over the cake, using the palms of your hands dusted with icing sugar. Smooth and trim any excess. Add more pink colouring to the leftover icing to tint it darker pink and wrap in plastic.
3 Insert 4 skewers into the cake to support the layers (see page 9).

Knead 2¹/₂ packets of the icing and tint pale blue. Roll out to cover the 25 cm (10 inch) cake. Tint the leftover icing darker blue. Repeat the process with the skewers.
4 Knead 1¹/₂ packets of icing and tint pale yellow to cover the 16 cm (6¹/₂ inch) cake. Keep a little pale icing and tint the rest darker. Repeat the process with the skewers.
5 Knead 1 packet of the icing and tint pale orange to cover the smallest cake. Tint the leftover icing darker orange.
6 Place the cakes on top of each other. Roll the darker icing out on an icing sugar dusted surface to about 3 mm (¹/₈ inch) thick. Cut small hearts from the pink icing and stick onto the pink cake with a little egg white. Cut strips from the blue icing and stick onto the blue cake. Using a cutter or knife, cut daisy shapes from the dark yellow icing and stick onto the yellow cake—cut small rounds from the pale yellow icing for the centres. Stick small dots of dark orange icing to the orange cake. Re-roll the remaining dark orange icing and cut into 3 cm (1¹/₄ inch) wide strips; stick to the cake to form a flat ribbon. Re-roll the remaining icing and cut 2 strips. Trim the ends as shown (step photograph 3), fold in half and support with cotton wool. Wrap a small strip of icing over the centre of the join for the centre of the bow. Place in the centre of the 'ribbon'. Remove the cotton wool when set.

Ahead of time: Can be kept for 2 weeks. You could use all fruit cake layers and store for 1 year.

To cover the cake, roll the icing over the pin, then reroll over the top of the cake.

Cut out tiny daisies from the darker yellow icing and stick them to the cake with egg white.

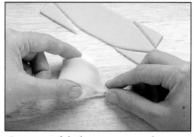

Cut strips of dark orange icing, then trim the corners and fold in half.

Wrap a small strip of icing over the centre of the join to make a bow.

Toffee circles
Making toffee shapes is fun, but don't attempt it on a very hot day or you might have problems with your toffee circles softening and not looking their best.

four 9 cm (3¹/2 inch) round
  cakes (we used carrot cake,
  but you could use butter or
  coconut cake)

Cream cheese frosting
375 g (13 oz) cream cheese
75 g (2¹/2 oz) unsalted butter
90 g (3 oz) icing sugar, sifted
1 teaspoon vanilla essence

100 g (3¹/2 oz) caster sugar
ground nutmeg, to dust

1 To make the frosting, beat the cream cheese and butter with electric beaters until smooth and creamy. Gradually beat in the icing sugar and vanilla essence, beating until thick and creamy. Divide the frosting into four portions and spread the top and side of each cake with a portion. Spread the frosting over the cakes roughly; it does not need to be smooth.

2 To make the toffee, place a heavy-based pan over medium heat, gradually sprinkle with some of the caster sugar and, as it melts, sprinkle with the remaining sugar. Stir to melt any lumps and prevent the sugar burning. When the toffee is golden brown, remove the pan from the heat. Line a couple of baking trays with foil. Using a wooden spoon, drizzle toffee circles on the lined trays, then leave until the toffee has set completely.

3 Sprinkle the top of each cake lightly with a little nutmeg. Arrange a toffee circle on each cake just before serving.

Ahead of time: The cakes can be iced up to 2 days in advance and kept in the fridge or in an airtight container in a cool dark place. The toffee circles can be made up to a day in advance and kept in a single layer, between baking paper, in an airtight container. Don't put the toffee on the cake until just before serving or it will soften and begin to turn sticky.

Spread a portion of frosting over the top and side of each cake.

As the sugar melts, sprinkle more sugar on top of it, stirring to melt the lumps.

Drizzle the toffee in circles over the lined baking tray and leave to set.

Star of the show

Chocolate, toffee and truffles... this is a 21st cake for someone really special. If you don't have a cake board big enough you could use a large clean tile or covered chopping board.

one 30 cm (12 inch) square mud cake

50 x 40 cm (20 x 16 inch) covered cake board
icing sugar, for dusting

Chocolate glaze
500 g (1 lb) dark chocolate
330 g (11 oz) sugar

Truffles
60 ml (2 fl oz) brandy
200 g (6¹/₂ oz) dark chocolate, melted
60 g (2 oz) raisins, finely chopped
140 g (4¹/₂ oz) roasted hazelnuts, chopped
dark cocoa powder

Toffee
660 g (1 lb 5 oz) caster sugar

1 Make a triangular cardboard template and cut away the sides of the cake as shown (step photograph 1). Place the cake on the board and use part of the sides to build up the top part of the cake into a large triangle. Keep the leftover cake.
2 To make the chocolate glaze, chop the chocolate and put in a pan with the sugar and 250 ml (8 fl oz) water. Stir over low heat until blended and dissolved. Bring to the boil, then reduce the heat slightly. Boil for 6–8 minutes, stirring occasionally to prevent burning. Remove from the heat and stir gently to cool slightly. Pour evenly over the cake (don't wash the pan,

you'll need the leftover glaze). When the glaze has set, trim any drips off the board.
3 To make the truffles, crumble the reserved cake and measure 900 g (1 lb 14 oz) of cake crumbs into a large bowl. Mix with the brandy, dark chocolate and raisins. Roll into balls, using 2 level teaspoons for each ball. Roll half the balls in the hazelnuts and the rest in cocoa. Refrigerate on paper-covered trays.
4 Cover 3 oven trays with non-stick baking paper. Place a heavy-based frying pan over medium heat, gradually sprinkle with 250 g (8 oz) of the sugar and, as it melts, sprinkle with more sugar. Stir to melt any lumps and prevent burning. When golden brown, remove from the heat. Pour onto the trays and carefully spread with a wooden spoon. Using a tea towel (the trays will become very hot), tilt the trays to spread the toffee as thinly as possible. Leave until cold.
5 Break the toffee into jagged pieces and stick to the cake sides, using the leftover warm glaze. Place the truffles around the edge of the cake, (you might need to reroll the cocoa covered balls) securing them to the board with glaze. Serve any leftover truffles separately. Cut stars out of the template, hold over the cake and dust with icing sugar.

Ahead of time:
The glazed cake will keep for 3 days. The truffles will keep for 2 weeks. The toffee is best made closer to serving

Make a template and trim away triangles from the sides of the cake.

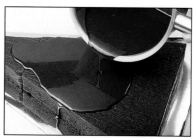

Pour the glaze evenly over the cake. When it has set, remove any drips.

Melt some of the sugar, then sprinkle with more, stirring all the time.

Spread toffee onto each of the trays, then tilt the tray to spread the toffee thinly.

Cut stars out of the template and sprinkle icing sugar through the holes.

Berry cake

Build up your layers of cake, spread with a meringue frosting and then top with whatever's in season. Pile your favourite berries high for a touch of fruity glamour.

two 20 cm (8 inch) round cakes (we used coconut cake, but you could use chocolate or butter cake)

Meringue frosting
3 egg whites
165 g (5½ oz) caster sugar
250 g (8 oz) unsalted butter

110 g (3½ oz) caster sugar
3 tablespoons Cointreau or orange juice
750 g (1½ lb) assorted fresh berries (blueberries, raspberries, blackberries or loganberries)

1 To make the meringue frosting, put the egg whites and sugar in a heatproof bowl. Bring a small pan of water to a simmer and place the bowl over the pan (don't let the base of the bowl sit in the water). Stir to dissolve the sugar, but be careful not to cook the egg whites.
2 When the sugar has dissolved, remove from the heat and beat with electric beaters for 5 minutes, or until stiff peaks form. Cut the butter into about 10 pieces and add, piece by piece, beating after each addition. The mixture should thicken when you have a couple of pieces of butter left, but continue until you have added it all.
3 Put the sugar in a small pan with 185 ml (6 fl oz) water and stir over the heat until the sugar has dissolved. Stir in the Cointreau.
4 Trim the domed top off each cake to give a flat surface. Slice each cake in half horizontally and place one layer on a serving plate or board. Brush well with the Cointreau syrup and spread with a thin layer of frosting. Repeat this to build up the layers, finishing with a layer of cake.
5 Spread the remaining frosting evenly over the top and side of the cake with a palette or flat-bladed knife. Spread the frosting up the side of the cake to make furrows. Pile the berries on top of the cake. Dust with a little icing sugar if you prefer your berries sweetened.

Ahead of time: The cake can be iced up to a day in advance, but don't add the berries until you are ready to serve.

Note: If you prefer, use a white chocolate ganache instead of the frosting: put 150 g (5 oz) white chocolate melts, 130 g (4½ oz) chopped white chocolate, 125 ml (4 fl oz) cream and 250 g (8 oz) butter in a pan and stir over low heat until melted and smooth. Transfer to a small bowl, cover the surface with plastic wrap and leave overnight to cool. Beat with electric beaters for 3–5 minutes, or until thick, pale and creamy.

Stir the egg whites and sugar to dissolve the sugar without cooking the egg whites.

Brush with the syrup, spread with a layer of frosting, then repeat the layers.

Spread the frosting up the side of the cake to make furrows.

Peach and orange mousse cake

This cake is perfect for just about any summery special occasion. Peaches were

our fancy but you could use other stone fruits that are in season.

one 20 cm (8 inch) round cake
(we used coconut cake, but
you could use butter cake)

shiny contact

Mousse
150 g (5 oz) white chocolate,
   chopped
150 g (5 oz) cream cheese
60 g (2 oz) caster sugar
80 ml (2³/4 fl oz) orange juice
3 teaspoons gelatine
300 ml (10 fl oz) cream,
   whipped
2 egg whites, whipped to soft
   peaks

Topping
125 ml (4 fl oz) fresh strained
   orange juice
1 tablespoon caster sugar
³/4 teaspoon gelatine
1 large peach, cut into wedges

1 Slice the cake in half
horizontally. Lightly grease a deep
20 cm (8 inch) springform tin. Cut
a piece of shiny contact about 2 cm
(1 inch) higher than the tin and
wrap around the inside of the tin as
a collar. Put half of the cake in the
tin (you won't need the other half,
so freeze for next time or make
truffles). Pull the contact tight and
secure with a paper clip and tape.
2 To make the mousse, bring a
pan with a little water to a simmer,
then remove from the heat. Place
the chocolate in a heatproof bowl,
then place the bowl over the pan.

Don't let the bowl sit in the water.
Stir the chocolate until melted. Beat
the cream cheese and sugar until
smooth and creamy, then beat in
the cooled melted chocolate. Heat
the orange juice in a small pan and
remove from the heat. Sprinkle with
the gelatine and stir until dissolved.
Cool slightly before beating into the
cream cheese mixture. Fold in the
cream, then the softly whipped egg
whites. Pour the mousse over the
cake base and gently tap the tin on
the bench to level the surface. Chill
for several hours or until firm.
3 To make the topping, put the
orange juice and sugar in a small
pan. Stir over low heat until the
sugar has dissolved. Sprinkle with
the gelatine and continue stirring
until it has dissolved. Remove from
the heat and leave to cool. Arrange
the sliced peach on top of the
mousse. Carefully pour the topping
over the cake. Refrigerate for several
hours, or until the topping has
completely set, before removing the
cake from the tin. Carefully pull
away the contact.

Ahead of time: Can be kept,
covered, in the fridge for 3 days.

Note: If fresh peaches aren't
available, use very well-drained
canned peaches.

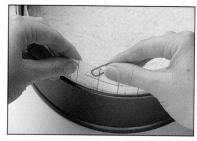

*Pull the contact tight so that the mousse
will set completely in line with the cake.*

*Fold the softly whipped egg whites into the
mousse mixture.*

*Arrange the peach slices on top of the
cake, then pour over the topping.*

Floodwork flowers *Transform a simple cake into*

a work of art, using the floodwork technique. All you need is a palette of coloured

icing and a little imagination.

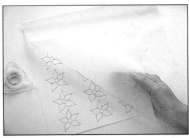

Draw the flowers on paper, tape to a work surface and cover with baking paper.

one 18 x 25 cm (7 x 10 inch) oval cake (we used mud cake, but you could use butter, chocolate or coconut cake)

Floodwork flowers

1 egg white
250 g (8 oz) pure icing sugar
3 teaspoons lemon juice
assorted food colourings

White chocolate buttercream

80 ml (2³/4 fl oz) cream
150 g (5 oz) white chocolate melts
200 g (6¹/2 oz) unsalted butter
80 g (2³/4 oz) icing sugar

1 To make the flowers, lightly beat the egg white with a wooden spoon. Gradually add the sifted icing sugar and beat to a smooth paste. Gradually add 2 teaspoons lemon juice until the mixture has a slightly stiff piping consistency (not too runny). Cover the surface with plastic wrap to stop it drying out.
2 Draw 16 simple flowers on a sheet of paper and tape this to a flat work surface. Tape a sheet of baking paper over the top of the drawing sheet. Using a 1 mm piping nozzle, pipe carefully over the outlines. Remove the baking paper sheet and set aside to dry. Repeat with a second sheet of baking paper.
3 Gradually add more lemon juice to the icing until it is slightly thinner and will spread smoothly. Divide the icing into 4 bowls and add a different colour to each (keep

the bowls covered or the icing will dry out quickly). Using paper piping bags, pipe the icing inside the flower outlines. Place the sheets on baking trays and dry overnight.
4 To make the buttercream, bring a little water in a pan to a simmer and remove from the heat. Put the cream and chocolate in a heatproof bowl and place over the pan (not touching the water). Stir until smooth, then allow to cool slightly. Beat the butter until light and creamy, then slowly beat in the icing sugar until thick and white. Beat in the cool chocolate mixture.
5 Cut the dome off the cake and put the cake upside down on a serving plate. Spread two thirds of the buttercream over the cake, smoothing the surface. Carefully lift the flowers off the baking paper with a palette knife (be very careful as they break easily). Press the flowers around the top edge of the cake, so they stand up slightly higher than the cake. Arrange the remainder in a bunch in the centre.
6 Tint some of the remaining buttercream pink and the rest green. Using a paper piping bag, pipe green stems down from the flowers on the side of the cake and from the bunch in the centre. To make pointed leaves, cut the tip of the bag into a 'v', press firmly, then pull away. Pipe a pink bow in the middle of the bunch of flowers.

Ahead of time: The cake will keep for 3 days after icing. The flowers can be made up to a week in advance: when dry, store in a single layer in an airtight container.

Pipe the white icing around the outlines of the flowers, using a fine nozzle.

With the thicker, coloured icing fill in the petals and centres of the flowers.

The floodwork flowers are fragile so use a palette knife to gently remove them.

Cut a 'v' in the tip of the piping bag to make pointed leaves on the stems.

Saint Valentine's day *This Valentine's day,*

don't keep it a secret... let your loved one know what you really think of them with

this spectacular cake. You could also try a deep vibrant red icing or hearts.

one 20 cm (8 inch) round cake
(we used butter cake, but you
could use chocolate, or
coconut cake)

Pink buttercream
50 g (1³/4 oz) unsalted butter
120 g (4 oz) icing sugar, sifted
3 teaspoons liqueur (Cointreau,
Grand Marnier etc)
a few drops of red food
colouring

500 g (1 lb) soft icing (ready-
made or see page 7)
icing sugar

1 Draw round the base of the cake
tin and cut out a 20 cm (8 inch)
circle from a piece of paper. Fold
the circle in half and draw on half a
heart shape using the fold as the
middle of the heart and the outside
edge as the edge of the heart. Cut
along this line and unfold the paper
to make a heart-shaped template.
2 Cut the domed top off the cake
to give a flat surface. Turn the cake
upside down and use the template
to cut into a heart with a serrated
knife. The cake should cut easily
and leave a clean edge.
3 To make the pink buttercream,
beat the butter until soft, add the
sifted sugar and continue beating
until light and fluffy. Add the
liqueur and colouring and beat well.
4 Cut the cake in half
horizontally. Spread the bottom
layer with a third of the buttercream
and sandwich the halves together.

Spread the remaining buttercream
over the cake in a thin layer, to help
the next layer of icing stick. Place
the cake on a serving plate or board.
5 Knead the icing until smooth on
a surface dusted with icing sugar.
Add a couple of drops of food
colouring and knead into the icing
until it is pale pink (you may need
to add more icing sugar as you go
along). Pull off a piece the size of a
golf ball and add another few drops
of food colouring to make it darker.
Continue doing this until you have
three or four different shades of
pink icing set aside. Roll out the
remaining icing into a circle large
enough to cover the top and side of
the cake. Carefully drape this over
the cake, easing it into the corners
and around the edges until it fits
snugly all over. As long as you don't
over-roll your icing you should not
have any folds or pleats—if you do
then just smooth them in. Trim
away any excess and set it aside.
6 Roll out the balls of coloured
icing and stamp out heart shapes
using varying sized cutters. If you
want any of the hearts to be red,
paint them with the food colouring
and leave to dry. Mix 1 tablespoon
of icing sugar with a little water to
make a runny paste and use a tiny
dab of this to stick each heart onto
the cake.

Ahead of time: This cake will
keep for up to 3 days in an airtight
container after icing.

Fold the paper circle in half, draw half a heart on one side and cut out.

Put the paper template over the cake and cut with a serrated knife.

Ease the icing into the corners and around the edges until it fits snugly.

Roll out the balls of coloured icing and cut out heart shapes of different sizes.

Raspberry tuiles cake *A traditional French*

biscuit, 'tuile' is French for 'tile'. These deliciously thin wafers are piled on top of

our frosted cake. The scattered fresh raspberries give a subtle hint of colour.

one 20 cm (8 inch) square cake
(we used butter cake, but
you could use carrot or
coconut cake)

Tuiles
1 plastic lid for template
1 egg white
30 g (1 oz) icing sugar
2 tablespoons plain flour
30 g (1 oz) unsalted butter,
melted
1/2 teaspoon vanilla essence
250 g (8 oz) raspberries

Cream cheese frosting
250 g (8 oz) cream cheese
50 g (1³/4 oz) butter
1 teaspoon vanilla essence
60 g (2 oz) icing sugar, sifted

1 Preheat the oven to moderate 180°C (350°F/Gas 4). To make the tuiles, line 2 oven trays with baking paper. Make the plastic lid into a template by cutting 2 triangles from the centre of it: each of the triangles should measure 10 x 10 x 4 cm (4 x 4 x 1¹/2 inches). Beat the egg white into soft peaks with electric beaters. Gradually add the icing sugar, beating well after each addition. Stir in the flour, then add the butter and vanilla and stir until the mixture is smooth.

2 Place the template on the lined baking tray and spread a little of the mixture evenly into the triangles with a palette knife. Lift off the template and bake the tuiles for 3–4 minutes, or until lightly golden. (Don't bake more than a couple at a time, as they set quickly and you need to give yourself time to remove and mould them.) Leave on the tray for 10–15 seconds, then, working quickly, carefully loosen the tuiles and drape over a rolling pin or jar until cool. As you bake the rest of the mixture, cool the tuiles over different sized curved objects to vary their shapes.

3 To make the frosting, beat the cream cheese and butter with electric beaters until light and creamy. Add the vanilla essence, then gradually beat in the icing sugar until light and fluffy.

4 Place the cake on a serving plate. Spread the icing over the top and side, making swirls and peaks with a palette knife. Arrange the tuiles and raspberries over the top.

Ahead of time: The cake can be iced up to a day in advance and kept refrigerated—let it come back to room temperature before serving. The tuiles are best made on the day and added just before serving.

Note: If you prefer, use a white chocolate ganache instead of the frosting: put 150 g (5 oz) white chocolate melts, 130 g (4¹/2 oz) chopped white chocolate, 125 ml (4 fl oz) cream and 250 g (8 oz) butter in a pan and stir over low heat until melted and smooth. Transfer to a small bowl, cover the surface with plastic wrap and leave overnight to cool. Beat with electric beaters for 3–5 minutes, or until thick, pale and creamy.

Use the lid from a plastic container to make a triangular template.

Use a palette knife to spread the tuile mixture over the template triangles.

Loosen the tuiles from the paper and drape over curved objects to cool.

Marble glazed cake *The secret to a good marbled*

finish is not to mix your icings together too thoroughly. Simply spoon them over

the cake, then swirl together gently with a skewer.

two 20 cm (8 inch) round cakes
(we used chocolate cake, but
you could use mud cake)

White chocolate buttercream

4 tablespoons cream
150 g (5 oz) white chocolate
melts
200 g (6^1/$_2$ oz) unsalted butter
80 g (2^3/$_4$ oz) icing sugar

80 g (2^3/$_4$ oz) milk chocolate
125 ml (4 fl oz) cream
80 g (2^3/$_4$ oz) dark chocolate
80 g (2^3/$_4$ oz) white chocolate
200 g (6^1/$_2$ oz) flaked almonds,
toasted

1 To make the white chocolate
buttercream, put the cream and
chocolate in a small heatproof bowl.
Bring a small pan of water to a
simmer, remove from the heat and
place the bowl over the pan (don't
let the bottom of the bowl sit in the
water). Stir the chocolate over the
hot water until melted, then remove
from the heat and leave to cool.
Chop the butter and beat until light
and creamy, then gradually beat in
the sugar until thick and white. Beat
in the melted chocolate until the
mixture is thick and fluffy.
2 Using a serrated knife, cut each
cake horizontally into 3 even layers
(trim away the domed top, if
necessary). Place a layer of cake on a
wire rack over a tray and spread
with a sixth of the buttercream. Top
with another layer of cake, spread

that with buttercream and build up
the layers, sandwiching the cake
and filling. Finish with a layer of
cake, cut-side-down to give a flat
surface (keep the remaining portion
of buttercream). Refrigerate the cake
for 30 minutes to firm the filling, so
that the layers don't slide apart.
3 Put the milk chocolate in a small
heatproof bowl with 2 tablespoons
of the cream. Bring a small pan of
water to a simmer, remove from the
heat and place the bowl over the
pan (don't let the bottom of the
bowl sit in the water). Stir the
chocolate and cream over the hot
water until melted and blended.
Alternatively, melt in the microwave
for 1 minute on High, stirring after
30 seconds. Do the same with the
dark chocolate and white chocolate,
blending each with 2 tablespoons
cream so you have three separate
chocolate mixtures.
4 Spoon dollops of each chocolate
mixture randomly over the top of
the cake and then swirl them
together with the thick end of a
skewer to create a marbling effect.
Gently tap the tray on the bench to
level the icing. Leave to set, then
remove any drips of icing from
down the side of the cake and
spread the remaining buttercream
around the side. Roughly crush the
almonds and press over the
buttercream. Transfer the cake to a
serving plate or stand.

Ahead of time: This cake can
be stored in the fridge for up to
3 days after decorating. Bring to
room temperature before serving.

*Stand the cake on a rack over a tray and
build up layers of cake and buttercream.*

*Melt the three chocolates separately and
then dollop over the top of the cake.*

*Gently swirl together the coloured
chocolates, to give a marbled effect.*

Striped cake with mango *The striped*

collar gives this cake a quirky character, while the mango adds an irresistible taste

of summer. If mangoes are not in season, use fresh peaches or strawberries.

two 22 cm (9 inch) round classic
 sponge cakes

Sponge collar

3 eggs, separated
135 g (4^1/$_2$ oz) caster sugar
60 g (2 oz) self-raising flour
3 tablespoons cornflour
30 g (1 oz) butter, melted
1^1/$_2$ tablespoons cocoa powder

Chantilly cream

600 ml (20 fl oz) cream
2 teaspoons vanilla essence
30 g (1 oz) icing sugar

2 mangoes

1 Preheat the oven to moderate
180°C (350°F/Gas 4). To make the
sponge collar you will need to make
three lengths of striped sponge to
wrap around the cake (you would
need a very long baking tray to
make the collar in one section).
Draw three sets of two parallel lines
28 cm (11 inches) long and 7 cm
(3 inches) apart on a piece of baking
paper and place upside down on a
baking tray (you might need to use
two or three separate baking trays,
depending on their size). Beat the
egg whites until firm peaks form.
Gradually add the sugar, beating
well after each addition until the
sugar has dissolved and the mixture
is glossy. Beat in the egg yolks.
Using a metal spoon, fold in the
combined sifted flours and the
butter, until smooth. Divide the
mixture in half and fold the sifted
cocoa into one half.

2 Place the plain half of the
sponge mixture into a piping bag
fitted with a 1 cm (¹/₂ inch) nozzle.
On the baking paper, pipe lines at
1 cm (¹/₂ inch) intervals between
the three sets of parallel pencil lines
on the baking paper. Spoon the
cocoa mixture into a second bag
and pipe between the white sponge
lines. Bake for 5–8 minutes, or until
lightly browned. Leave the striped
sponge on the trays to cool. You
should have 3 striped sponge strips.

3 To make the chantilly cream,
beat the cream, vanilla essence and
icing sugar until soft peaks form.

4 Use a large serrated knife to slice
each sponge in half horizontally.
Sandwich together 3 layers of the
cake, using most of the chantilly
cream (keep some for the top and
side). Place the cake on a serving
plate (you will not be using the final
layer of cake, but it can be frozen or
used for cake crumbs). Trim one
edge of each sponge collar to make
them the same height as the cake.
Cover the side of the cake with a
thin layer of the chantilly cream and
spread the remainder on top.
Carefully place the sponge collars
around the side of the cake—
putting the flat side against the cake
and the cut edge at the base.

5 Peel the mangoes and cut into
slices. Fan over the top of the cake
before serving.

Ahead of time: This cake is

best served on the day it is made.

Pipe the plain sponge mixture in rows between the pencil lines on the paper.

Pipe the chocolate sponge mixture between the plain sponge rows.

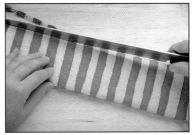

Trim the edge of the striped collar to make it the same height as the cake.

Gold leaf cake *What decadence! For a truly special occasion, edible gold leaf is the only thing to serve! This will really make your guests sit up and take notice.*

one 20 cm (8 inch) round cake (we used mud cake, but you could use chocolate cake)

Dark chocolate glaze
250 g (8 oz) dark chocolate, roughly chopped
125 g (4 oz) unsalted butter, chopped
2 teaspoons glycerine
2 teaspoons light corn syrup

24 carat edible gold leaf

1 Use a serrated knife to cut the dome off the top of the cake and level the surface. Turn the cake upside down on a wire rack, so that the flat base of the cake becomes the top. Stand the wire rack on a tray, to catch any glaze that may drip.
2 To make the dark chocolate glaze, put the chocolate, butter, glycerine and corn syrup in a small pan. Stir over low heat until melted and smooth. Alternatively you can make the glaze in a heatproof bowl in the microwave oven: melt on High for 1–2 minutes, stirring at 30 second intervals, until smooth.
3 Pour the chocolate glaze over the cake, allowing it to completely cover the side. Leave in a cool place until the glaze has set completely, then carefully lift onto a serving plate or cake board. Use tweezers or a small brush to remove the gold leaf from the sheets and stick randomly over the cake. If the gold leaf won't stick to the glaze, dab a little egg white onto the glaze first, then stick the gold leaf to it.

Ahead of time: The cake can be decorated up to 3 days in advance and stored in an airtight container in the fridge—allow the cake to return to room temperature before serving.

Note: Edible gold leaf is available from art supply shops and some cake decorating shops. You will need 1–2 sheets for this recipe. You might need to buy several sheets in a pack, but it will keep indefinitely.

Slice the domed top off the cake to give a flat surface. Then turn upside down.

Pour the chocolate glaze over the cake, letting it run down to cover the side.

Remove pieces of gold leaf from the sheet with tweezers and stick to the cake.

Christmas cake *Use our rich fruit cake recipe and you*

can do your baking and decorating up to two months before Christmas and rest

assured that your cake will taste even better than the day it came out of the oven.

one 22 cm (9 inch) round fruit
cake

2 tablespoons apricot jam
400 g (13 oz) almond icing
(ready-made or see page 6)
500 g (1 lb) pure icing sugar
3 egg whites, lightly beaten
25 cm (10 inch) round cake
board
200 g (6$^{1}/_{2}$ oz) ready-made soft
icing (or use the recipe on
page 7)
green and red food colouring
ribbon

1 Trim the dome from the top of
the cake to give a flat surface. Turn
the cake upside down. Melt the jam
in a small pan, strain and brush
over the surface of the cake, to
make the almond icing stick. Knead
the almond icing on a work surface
dusted with icing sugar until it is
smooth. Roll out large enough to
cover the cake. Lift the almond icing
carefully onto the cake, smoothing
it down the side to prevent any
folds. Trim neatly around the base
and smooth with the palms of your
hands dusted with icing sugar. Dry
overnight in a cool dry place.
2 Sift the icing sugar into a large
bowl, making sure there are no
lumps. Make a well in the centre
and add the egg whites, stirring
from the centre outwards until
completely mixed in. The mixture
will be fairly stiff. Beat with an
electric hand mixer until fluffy—it
should be spreadable but not runny.

3 Secure the cake to the cake
board with a little icing. Spoon
about a third of the icing on top and
spread out to the edge of the cake
with a palette knife. If you have one,
use a steel ruler to smooth the
surface: hold each side of the ruler
and pull it towards you over the
icing (you may need to do this a few
times, adding more icing if
necessary). Ice the side of the cake
with a palette knife or ruler. If you
have a turn- table, this will make
everything easier. If not, place your
cakeboard on top of the upturned
cake tin that you have just used, to
give you a little more height and
make turning the cake easier. When
you have as smooth a surface as
possible, leave the cake to dry. (If
you want to create a snow scene
then, using the end of the palette
knife, press down and lift at
intervals all over the icing, to make
peaks.) Keep a little icing, covered
with plastic wrap.
4 Roll out the soft icing on a work
surface dusted with icing sugar and
cut out leaf shapes with cutters or
by hand. Leave to dry, either flat or
over a rolling pin to make them
curve slightly, then paint different
shades of green. Roll a few holly
berries and paint them red when
dry. Decorate the cake with a
wreath of leaves, attaching each one
with a dab of icing, and add a few
berries. Tie with a ribbon to serve
and dust lightly with icing sugar.

Ahead of time: The decorated
cake can be stored for 2 months in
an airtight container in a cool place.

*Roll out the almond icing, then lift onto
the cake and smooth down the sides.*

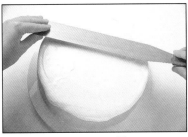

*Spread the icing as smoothly as you can,
using a palette knife or metal ruler.*

*A turntable will make it easier to ice the
cake, otherwise place it on top of the tin.*

*It is worth investing in some leaf cutters to
give a really neat finish.*

Sweet fig and chocolate cake

This glamorously understated cake is perfect for a sophisticated occasion where style and taste are the most important items on the menu.

one 20 cm (8 inch) round cake (we used butter cake, but you could use chocolate, mud or coconut cake)

Buttercream
250 g (8 oz) unsalted butter
125 g (4 oz) icing sugar, sifted
1 teaspoon vanilla essence
2 teaspoons milk

Kirsch or other fruit-based liqueur
4 tablespoons raspberry jam
300 g (10 oz) white chocolate melts
5 fresh figs, quartered

1 To make the buttercream, beat the butter with electric beaters until light and creamy. Gradually add the icing sugar alternately with the vanilla essence and milk, beating until smooth and fluffy.

2 Use a serrated knife to slice the cake horizontally into 3 even layers. Place the bottom layer on a board or plate. Brush with a little liqueur and spread with half the jam. Spread with a thin layer of buttercream. Place another cake layer on top and repeat the layers. Top with the remaining cake layer, and spread the rest of the buttercream evenly over the cake.

3 Put the white chocolate melts in a heatproof bowl. Bring a small pan of water to a simmer, remove from the heat and place the bowl over the pan (don't let the bottom of the bowl sit in the water). Stir the chocolate until melted. (Or melt in the microwave for 1 minute on High, stirring after 30 seconds.)

4 Spread the melted chocolate in 5 x 11 cm (2 x 5 inch) strips over a sheet of baking paper. Leave to set completely before removing from the paper—you will need about 20 of these shapes but make a few extra in case of breakages. Break one end of each strip or trim with a knife to give a flat base, then stand them upright around the edge of the cake, slightly overlapping. You can tie a ribbon around the cake or leave it plain. Arrange the fresh fig quarters around the edge.

Ahead of time: This cake can be decorated up to 2 days in advance, but add the figs just before serving. Keep in a cool dark place in an airtight container or in the fridge in warm weather.

Brush the cake with liqueur, spread with jam and then with buttercream.

Spread the melted white chocolate in strips over a sheet of baking paper.

Break the end off each strip of chocolate, to give a flat base to stand it up on.

Wrapped presents *Add ribbon to make these cakes*

into birthday 'parcels', or white flowers to transform them into wonderful

individual wedding cakes.

one 23 cm (9 inch) square cake
(we used mud cake, but you
could use fruit cake)

2 tablespoons apricot jam
500 g (1 lb) almond icing (use
ready-made or see page 6)
pure icing sugar
1 egg white
500 g (1 lb) soft icing (use
ready-made or see page 7)
ribbon and fresh flowers

1 Trim the edges of the cake neatly and cut into quarters to make four small square cakes. Turn the cakes upside down, so the neat bases become the tops. Heat the jam until runny, strain and brush all over the cakes to make the almond icing stick. Knead the almond icing until smooth on a work surface lightly dusted with icing sugar. Divide the almond icing into four and roll out one portion large enough to cover the top and sides of one cake. Carefully mould over the cake, smoothing the top and sides with the palms of your hands dusted with icing sugar, and trim the edges. Repeat with the rest of the almond icing and cakes.

2 Brush the egg white over the almond icing to make the soft icing stick to the cakes. Divide the soft icing into four portions. Knead until just pliable, then roll out each portion large enough cover one of the cakes. Mould over the cakes as before and trim the edges. Leave the icing to dry for at least 24 hours before decorating.

3 Decorate two of the cakes with ribbon bows and two with flowers. Mix a little of the egg white and some sifted icing sugar to make a paste. This will be used to glue the ribbon and flowers to the icing. For the ribbon-decorated cakes, cut two lengths of ribbon long enough to reach from one side of the cake to the other, crossing over the top, and secure in place with a little paste. Cut another length of ribbon and tie into a bow, sticking with a little paste. Secure the ribbon with pins while the paste sets, then stick the bow on the top of the cake.

4 For the flower-decorated cakes, wrap a length of ribbon around the base of the cake and attach with the paste, securing with pins until set. Cut the long stems from the flowers and arrange in a small bunch on top of the cake, sticking with a little paste. Remove the pins from the ribbon as soon as the paste has set.

Ahead of time: These cakes
can be iced and decorated with ribbon up to 2 weeks in advance. Store in an airtight container in a cool, dry place. Decorate with fresh flowers just before serving.

Trim the edges of the cake and cut neatly into four smaller square cakes.

Mould the icing over the cakes, smoothing with your hands. Trim the excess icing.

Mix a little egg white and icing sugar together to make a 'glue' for the ribbon.

Decorate a couple of cakes with ribbon and a couple with fresh flowers.

Wedding flowers *We've shown you a continental and*

a traditional cake—Wedding flowers is a modern cake for a less formal wedding.

Give the flower petals a marbled effect by not kneading the colouring in thoroughly.

one 22 cm (9 inch) round and
  one 18 cm (7 inch) round
  mud cake

1 quantity modelling paste (use
  ready-made or see page 7)
caramel food colouring
cornflour
petal shaped cutters
cake decorating wire
1 egg white

Meringue frosting
3 egg whites
165 g (5½ oz) caster sugar
250 g (8 oz) unsalted butter

1 To make the flowers, divide the modelling paste in half and tint one half pale cream. Don't knead evenly—leave the paste slightly streaky. Use small pieces of paste at a time and keep the rest tightly wrapped in plastic. Dust the bench with cornflour. Roll out the paste to 2 mm thick. Cut out 1 or 2 petals with a small cutter or sharp knife. Smooth the cut edges with your fingertips to thin them. Bend a piece of wire to make a small closed hook at one end. Lightly brush a little egg white on the end of the petal and fold the petal around the bent wire.
2 Repeat with a second petal, slightly overlapping the first. Continue, making the petals slightly larger as you go: either cut larger or roll them larger after cutting. Wrap up to 6 or 7 petals around the wire—give them a slight twist every so often to make them realistic. Put the flower in a padded egg carton, gently folding the wire so it sits evenly, while making the others.

3 When the first flower has dried, add more petals to make it larger. The paste will dry fast, so always work quickly with small portions. If you want, ruffle the edges with your fingertips or a decorating tool.
4 To make the meringue frosting, put the egg whites and sugar in a heatproof bowl. Bring a small pan of water to a simmer and place the bowl over the pan (don't let it sit in the water). Stir continuously to dissolve the sugar, but be careful not to cook the egg whites.
5 When the sugar has dissolved, remove the bowl from the top of the pan and beat the mixture with electric beaters for 5 minutes, or until stiff peaks form. Cut the butter into about 10 pieces and add, piece by piece, beating after each addition. The mixture should thicken when you have about 2 pieces of butter left, but continue until you have added it all.
6 Trim the domed tops from the cakes to level the surfaces. Place the large cake on a board. Top with the smaller cake, sandwiching them together with a little frosting. Spread the remaining frosting smoothly over the whole cake. Cut the wires off the flowers, leaving a 2 cm (1 inch) stalk. Fold the wire under the flowers and arrange them on top. Don't forget that the flowers have wire in them, so must be removed before cutting.

Ahead of time: The cake can be iced up to 2 days in advance and kept refrigerated. The flowers can be made up to 2 weeks in advance and kept in an airtight container in a cool dry place. Put the flowers on the cake on the day of serving.

Cut out petals, brush with a little egg white and wrap around the bent wire.

Make the petals slightly larger by using a larger cutter, or rolling them out.

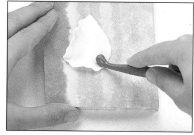

You can frill the edges of the petals with your fingers or a special decorating tool.

As you make the flowers, keep them safe in an egg box padded with cotton wool.

Cappuccino ice cream cake

Surprise everyone with your version of a cappuccino. The little chocolate spoon is

a delightful finishing touch.

Dissolve the instant coffee in the hot water, then mix into the ice cream.

one uncooked chocolate cake mixture from the recipe on page 11

1 tablespoon instant coffee powder
2 tablespoons boiling water
1 litre vanilla ice cream
250 ml (8 fl oz) thick cream
1 tablespoon icing sugar
125 g (4 oz) dark chocolate melts, melted
cocoa powder, for dusting

1 Preheat the oven to moderate 180°C (350°F/Gas 4). Lightly grease ten 1 cup (250 ml/8 fl oz) muffin holes with melted butter or oil. Divide the cake mixture evenly among the holes. Bake for about 25 minutes, or until a skewer comes out clean when inserted into the centre. Leave to cool in the tins for 5 minutes before turning onto a wire rack to cool completely.
2 Mix the coffee and water in a small bowl or cup until dissolved, then leave to cool. Roughly chop the ice cream in a large bowl and stir until thick and creamy. Add the coffee and stir until just combined. Return to the freezer until required. Beat the cream and icing sugar with electric beaters until soft peaks form. Refrigerate until required.
3 Draw the outlines of 10 small spoons onto baking paper, then turn the paper over. Spoon the chocolate into a paper piping bag, snip off the end and pipe around the outlines of the spoons, then fill in the outlines. You will need to

repeat this until you have piped 10 spoons. Allow to set.
4 Cut the top off each cake, leaving a 1 cm (1/2 inch) border around the top edge of each cake, reserving the tops. Scoop out the cake with a spoon, leaving a 1 cm (1/2 inch) thick shell of cake. (The leftover cake can be frozen for another use.)
5 Stir the coffee ice cream with a spoon to soften and spoon into the cakes, so that it comes slightly above the top of each cake. Replace the tops, pressing them down gently. Spread the beaten cream roughly over the tops of the cakes so that it looks like the froth on top of coffee. Dust lightly with the cocoa and serve with a chocolate spoon tucked in the cream.

Ahead of time: The ice cream can be prepared up to a week in advance, but allow it to soften a little before using. The finished cakes can be frozen, however the chocolate cake will not be quite as nice as when it's fresh. The chocolate spoons can be made up to 2 weeks in advance and stored in an airtight container.

Put the chocolate in a piping bag, pipe round the spoon then fill in the centre.

Cut the top off the cake, leaving a 1 cm border around the edge.

Use a spoon to scoop out the middle of the cake, leaving a 1 cm thick shell.

Spoon the ice cream into the cake, so it comes up over the top. Replace the lid.

Lemon curd meringue cake *Two*

old-fashioned favourites—lemon curd and meringue—are brought together to

make this spectacular cake with a distinctly modern touch.

two 22 cm (9 inch) round
  genoise sponges

4 egg whites
220 g (7 oz) caster sugar
pink food colouring
40 g (1½ oz) flaked almonds
250 ml (8 fl oz) thick cream
icing sugar, to dust

Lemon syrup
110 g (3½ oz) caster sugar
3 tablespoons lemon juice

Lemon curd
5 egg yolks
150 g (5 oz) caster sugar
1 tablespoon grated lemon rind
170 ml (5½ fl oz) lemon juice
180 g (6 oz) unsalted butter,
  chopped

1 Preheat the oven to slow 120°C (250°F/Gas ½). Cover 4 oven trays with non-stick baking paper. Mark a 21 cm (8½ inch) circle on 3 of the trays. Beat the egg whites into soft peaks. Gradually add the sugar, beating well after each addition until smooth and glossy. Tint the meringue pale pink with a little colouring. Spoon a quarter of the meringue into a piping bag fitted with a 1 cm (½ inch) plain nozzle. Pipe strips 1.5 cm (⅝ inch) apart along the length of the unmarked tray and sprinkle with the almonds. Spread the remaining meringue over the circles marked on the trays (they will spread slightly). Bake in two batches for 1 hour each; after

cooking, turn off the oven and leave to cool in the oven with the door ajar. Break each strip into 3 pieces and store in an airtight container for up to 2 days, until required.

2 For the lemon syrup, put the sugar and lemon juice in a small pan with 3 tablespoons water and stir over medium heat until the sugar has dissolved. Leave to cool.

3 To make the lemon curd, beat the egg yolks and sugar in a jug and strain into a heatproof bowl. Add the lemon rind, juice and butter and place the bowl over a pan of barely simmering water (don't let the bowl sit in the water). Stir over the heat for 20 minutes, or until the mixture thickens enough to coat the back of a spoon. Cool slightly then cover the surface with plastic wrap and leave until completely cold.

4 Cut the cakes in half horizontally. Place one layer on a plate, brush with the syrup and spread with a thin layer of lemon curd. Top with a round of meringue, trimming the edge to fit. Spread with lemon curd and top with another layer of cake. Repeat the layers, finishing with the last round of cake and syrup. Chill for several hours, at least, to soften the meringue.

5 Beat the cream into stiff peaks and spread over the cake. Pile the meringue fingers on the top and dust liberally with icing sugar.

Ahead of time: Ideally, make a
day in advance, to let the meringue soften. However, the decorated cake will not keep for longer than 2 days.

Pipe strips of pink meringue along the length of the baking tray.

Spread the remaining meringue over the circles marked on the baking trays.

Stir the lemon curd over the heat for 20 minutes, or until it coats a spoon.

Spread the cake with a layer of lemon curd, then top with a meringue circle.

Strawberries 'n' cream sponge with spun toffee *A great traditional favourite has*

been given a facelift with a little liqueur and a shimmering spun toffee topping.

two 22 cm (9 inch) round classic
  sponge cakes

750 ml (24 fl oz) cream
2 tablespoons icing sugar
500 g (1 lb) strawberries
Kirsch or Cointreau
250 g (8 oz) caster sugar

1 Using a serrated knife, slice each cake horizontally in half (you will only need 3 layers of cake, so freeze the remaining portion for trifles or cake crumbs). Whip the cream and icing sugar into stiff peaks. Hull half the strawberries and slice thinly.

2 Place one layer of cake on a serving plate or board and brush lightly with a little liqueur. Spread with a quarter of the cream and scatter with half the sliced strawberries. Repeat with another layer of cake, liqueur, cream and strawberries and refrigerate until the toffee is ready.

3 Put a heavy-based frying pan over medium heat, gradually sprinkle with some of the sugar and, as it melts, sprinkle with the remaining sugar. Stir to melt any lumps and prevent the sugar burning. When the toffee is golden brown, remove the pan immediately from the heat.

4 Spread the remaining cream roughly over the top of the cake. Arrange the remaining strawberries on top. Dip 2 forks in the toffee, then rub the backs of the forks together until the toffee begins to stick. Gently pull the forks apart to check whether the toffee is cool enough to spin. If it drips or dips, it probably needs a little longer to cool. If not, continue pulling the toffee apart over the cake, pressing the forks together to spin a second time when they meet. Re-dip and continue spinning backwards and forwards and over the cake. Serve immediately you've spun the toffee.

Ahead of time: The layered cake can be kept in the fridge for up to 2 hours before serving. Once you have spun the toffee over the top, serve immediately—the spun toffee will start to soften if left.

Once the toffee has turned golden brown, remove from the heat. Spin with 2 forks.

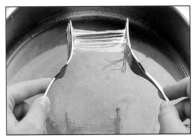

Gently pull the forks apart—if the toffee dips or drips it needs to cool longer.

Spin the toffee over the cake, pressing the forks together when they meet.

Coconut custard cake

Forget the fairground coconut shy—use your fresh coconut to create this eye-catching cake. Toast the coconut first to give a fabulous flavour.

Use a metal skewer to pierce two holes through the 'eyes' of the coconut.

Crack the coconut with a hammer, then remove chunks of flesh with a knife.

Use a sharp vegetable peeler to peel the coconut into strips.

Laying plastic wrap over the surface of the custard prevents a skin forming.

Press the toasted coconut shavings lightly over the meringue frosting.

two 20 cm (8 inch) square cakes (we used coconut cake, but you could use butter cake)

1 whole fresh coconut

Meringue frosting
3 egg whites
165 g (5^1/$_2$ oz) caster sugar
250 g (8 oz) unsalted butter

Custard
40 g (1^1/$_4$ oz) custard powder
90 g (3 oz) caster sugar
185 ml (6 fl oz) cream
315 ml (10 fl oz) milk
1 teaspoon vanilla essence

1 Preheat the oven to slow 150°C (300°F/Gas 2). Pierce 2 holes in one end of the coconut—use a metal skewer to pierce through the 'eyes'. Drain out the liquid, then crack the coconut open with a hammer and use a small knife to remove the flesh in large chunks. Leave the brown skin on the coconut flesh. Use a vegetable peeler to peel the coconut into long thin strips. Place the coconut strips on 2 oven trays and bake for 30–40 minutes, or until dry and lightly toasted. Turn the coconut during cooking so that it toasts evenly. Remove any coconut that has browned too much.

2 To make the meringue frosting, put the egg whites and sugar in a heatproof bowl. Bring a small pan of water to a simmer and place the bowl over the pan (don't let it sit in the water). Stir to dissolve the sugar, but don't cook the egg whites.

3 When the sugar has dissolved, remove from the heat and beat with electric beaters for 5 minutes, or until stiff peaks form. Cut the butter into about 10 pieces and add, piece by piece, beating after each addition. The mixture should thicken when you have about 2 pieces of butter left, but continue until you have added it all.

4 To make the custard, put the custard powder and sugar in a large pan. Whisk in the cream, milk and vanilla essence, then whisk over low heat until the mixture just boils and thickens. Remove from the heat and lay plastic wrap over the surface to stop a skin forming. Cool.

5 Slice each cake in half horizontally. Place one layer of cake on a serving plate. Beat the custard until smooth and spread a third over the cake, then top with another layer of cake. Continue layering, finishing with a layer of cake. Refrigerate for 1 hour.

6 Spread the meringue frosting roughly over the cake. Place the toasted coconut all over the cake, pressing lightly into the frosting.

Ahead of time: The cake can be layered with custard 2 days in advance and kept refrigerated. The toasted coconut can be kept in an airtight container for a day. The cake should be served within a few hours, once decorated, or the coconut will soften.

Daisy cake *Brighten up a special celebration with this sunny daisy cake—especially suitable for entertaining in the garden. Just looking at it will put a smile on everyone's face.*

two 20 cm (8 inch) round cakes (we used butter cake, but you could use coconut cake)

1 bunch of yellow daisies
1 egg white
caster sugar
3 tablespoons jam of your choice
yellow and green food colouring

Meringue frosting
3 egg whites
165 g (5½ oz) caster sugar
250 g (8 oz) unsalted butter

1 To frost the daisies, place the egg white in a shallow bowl and whisk until just foamy. Put some caster sugar on a large plate. Line a tray with paper towel. Trim the stalks from the daisies, making sure they are dry and unblemished. Working with one flower at a time, brush the egg white lightly over and between the petals, making sure the flower is completely coated but not too heavily. Sprinkle over the caster sugar, shake off any excess and dry on the lined tray. The drying time will depend on the humidity, but they could take up to an hour. It is very difficult to sugar flowers successfully if the weather is humid.
2 To make the meringue frosting, put the egg whites and sugar in a heatproof bowl. Bring a small pan of water to a simmer, remove from the heat and place the bowl over the pan (don't let the base of the bowl sit in the water). Stir continuously to dissolve the sugar, but be careful not to cook the egg whites.

3 When the sugar has dissolved, remove from the heat and beat with electric beaters for 3–5 minutes, or until stiff peaks form. Cut the butter into about 10 pieces and add, piece by piece, beating after each addition. The mixture should thicken when you have about two pieces of butter left, but continue until you have added it all.
4 Using a serrated knife, trim the domed tops from the cakes to give a flat surface. Place one cake, upside down, on a serving plate or cake board and sandwich to the other cake with 2 or 3 tablespoons of jam. Set aside about 3 tablespoons of the frosting and tint the remainder a very pale egg yellow. Spread the frosting evenly over the top and sides of the cake, using a palette or flat-bladed knife to make faint furrows up the side of the cake.
5 Tint the remaining frosting leaf green and spoon into a small icing bag fitted with a small plain nozzle. Pipe flower stems over the cake and attach a sugared daisy to the end of each stem. Snip a 'v' into the end of the piping bag to pipe little leaves onto the stems. Remove the daisies before eating!

Ahead of time: This cake can be decorated several hours in advance if kept in a cool, dry place. Sugared flowers do not keep well, so should be prepared on the day and, if necessary, kept in an airtight container in a cool dry place.

Brush over and between the petals with a little egg white, then sprinkle with sugar.

Spread the frosting evenly all over the cake and make furrows up the side.

Tint the frosting green and pipe flower stems over the cake.

Custard meringue gateau *The meringue*

ovals, moulded between two spoons, are called 'quenelles'. Here they've been

cleverly used to create a deliciously soft marshmallow border.

two 23 cm (9 inch) classic
   sponges

75 g (2¹/₂ oz) caster sugar
300 g (10 oz) raspberries, plus
   extra to decorate
90 g (3 oz) flaked almonds,
   toasted
2 tablespoons apricot jam
icing sugar, to dust

Custard filling
2 tablespoons custard powder
2 tablespoons cornflour
55 g (1³/₄ oz) caster sugar
1 teaspoon vanilla essence
500 ml (16 fl oz) milk
2 eggs, beaten

Meringue topping
4 egg whites
250 g (8 oz) caster sugar

1 Combine the sugar and 160 ml
(5¹/₂ fl oz) water in a small pan
and stir over medium heat until the
sugar has dissolved, then simmer
for 2 minutes. Allow to cool.
2 To make the custard filling,
blend the custard powder,
cornflour, sugar and vanilla in a pan
with a little of the milk to make a
smooth paste. Stir in the remaining
milk and eggs and mix well. Stir
over the heat until the mixture boils
and thickens. Pour into a large bowl
and cover the surface with plastic
wrap to prevent a skin forming. Stir
occasionally to cool the custard.
3 Slice each sponge in half
horizontally. Place one layer of
sponge on a lined oven tray. Brush

liberally with the cooled sugar
syrup. Beat the custard with a
wooden spoon to soften slightly.
Spread a third of the custard over
the cake, scatter with a third of the
raspberries, then top with more
cake. Build up the layers, finishing
with a layer of cake. Cover and chill
the cake for at least 1 hour.
4 Preheat the oven to very hot
250°C (500°F/Gas 10). Beat the egg
whites in a small bowl until stiff
peaks form. Gradually add the
sugar, beating well after each
addition until the sugar has
dissolved. Spread a thin layer of
meringue over the top and side of
the cake. Press the almonds all over
the side of the cake. Using two
dessert spoons, make small ovals
from the remaining meringue by
dipping the spoons quickly into
water, then scooping up a small
amount of meringue. Use the
second spoon to scoop the
meringue from the first spoon,
making an oval. Scoop gently off the
spoon around the edge of the cake.
5 Bake for 2–3 minutes, or until
the meringue is just brown on the
edges. You may need to turn the
cake halfway through cooking to
ensure even browning. Transfer to a
serving plate. Heat the apricot jam
in a small pan, push through a
strainer and gently brush over the
meringue ovals. Fill the centre of
the cake with fresh raspberries and
dust with icing sugar.

Ahead of time: The cake can
be stored for up to 2 days without
the meringue topping. Top with the
meringue on the day of serving.

*Make meringue ovals (quenelles) by
moulding with two dessert spoons.*

*Scoop the meringue off the spoon and
arrange around the edge of the cake.*

*Brush the meringue ovals with the
strained jam glaze.*

Helpful measures *Baking is one area of cookery where you really do need to be very precise in your measuring of ingredient quantities, tin sizes and oven temperatures. The following charts should give you all the information you need on cup and spoon measurements and conversions from metric to imperial.*

Because of the accuracy required when baking we have given ingredient measurements in metric and imperial in the recipes in this book, but not in cup measures. This is because, when using cup measures, we find that everybody will get a slightly different amount in their cup. Weighing scales will obviously give you more accurate and consistent measurements. Many people, however, find it convenient to use cup measurements or don't have scales. You can convert the metric or imperial measurements within the recipes into cup measures using the cup conversions chart below.

Standard measuring cups hold 250 ml (8 fl oz)—you can check an ordinary household cup for use by filling it with water and measuring the water.

We developed the recipes in this book in Australia where the tablespoon measure is 20 ml. In many other countries the tablespoon is 15 ml. For most recipes this difference will not be noticeable but, for recipes using baking powder, gelatine, bicarbonate of soda, small amounts of flour and cornflour, we suggest that, if you are using the smaller tablespoon, you add an extra teaspoon for each tablespoon.

OVEN TEMPERATURES

DESCRIPTION	°C	°F	GAS MARK
Very slow	120	250	$1/2$
	140	275	1
Slow	150	300	2
Warm	160	315	2–3
	170	325	3
Moderate	180	350	4
Moderately hot	190	375	5
	200	400	6
Hot	210	415	6–7
	220	425	7
Very hot	230	450	8
	240	475	9

LIQUID CUP MEASURES

$1/4$ cup	60 ml	2 fluid oz
$1/3$ cup	80 ml	$2^{3/4}$ fluid oz
$1/2$ cup	125 ml	4 fluid oz
$3/4$ cup	185 ml	6 fluid oz
1 cup	250 ml	8 fluid oz

SPOON MEASURES

$1/4$ teaspoon	1.25 ml
$1/2$ teaspoon	2.5 ml
1 teaspoon	5 ml
1 tablespoon	20 ml

CUP CONVERSIONS

1 cup plain/self-raising flour	125 g (4 oz)
1 cup butter	250 g (8 oz)
1 cup cocoa powder	125 g (4 oz)
1 cup cornflour	125 g (4 oz)
1 cup desiccated coconut	90 g (3 oz)
1 cup flaked coconut	60 g (2 oz)
1 cup currants	150 g (5 oz)
1 cup custard powder	125 g (4 oz)
1 cup chopped glacé fruit	240 g ($7^{1/2}$ oz)
1 cup grated chocolate	125 g (4 oz)
1 cup chopped chocolate	150 g (5 oz)
1 cup chocolate melts	150 g (5 oz)
1 cup choc bits	175 g (6 oz)
1 cup hazelnuts	140 g ($4^{1/2}$ oz)
1 cup chopped hazelnuts	120 g (4 oz)
1 cup ground hazelnuts	110 g ($3^{1/2}$ oz)
1 cup ground almonds	185 g (6 oz)
1 cup mixed peel	185 g (6 oz)
1 cup passionfruit pulp	250 g (8 oz)
1 cup raisins	125 g (4 oz)
1 cup sultanas	125 g (4 oz)
1 cup sugar, caster/granulated	250 g (8 oz)
1 cup icing sugar	125 g (4 oz)

WEIGHT		LENGTH		INTERNATIONAL INGREDIENT NAMES	
10 g	1/4 oz	5 mm	1/4 inch	baking tray	baking sheet
30 g	1 oz	1 cm	1/2 inch	bicarbonate of soda	baking soda
60 g	2 oz	2 cm	3/4 inch	choc bits	chocolate chips
90 g	3 oz	2.5 cm	1 inch	chocolate melts	chocolate buttons
125 g	4 oz	5 cm	2 inches	cornflour	cornstarch
150 g	5 oz	6 cm	2 1/2 inches	cream	single cream
185 g	6 oz	8 cm	3 inches	custard	custard sauce
220 g	7 oz	10 cm	4 inches	dark chocolate	plain/bittersweet
250 g	8 oz	12 cm	5 inches		chocolate
275 g	9 oz	15 cm	6 inches	flaked almonds	sliced almonds
300 g	10 oz	18 cm	7 inches	flaked coconut	coconut flakes
330 g	11 oz	20 cm	8 inches	golden syrup	light corn syrup
375 g	12 oz	23 cm	9 inches	greaseproof paper	waxed paper
400 g	13 oz	25 cm	10 inches	hazelnuts	filberts
425 g	14 oz	28 cm	11 inches	icing sugar	confectioners' sugar
475 g	15 oz	30 cm	12 inches	Madeira cake	pound cake
500 g	1 lb	35 cm	14 inches	mixed peel	mixed candied citrus rind
600 g	1 1/4 lb	46 cm	18 inches	plain flour	all-purpose flour
650 g	1 lb 5 oz	50 cm	20 inches	piping bag	decorating bag
750 g	1 1/2 lb	61 cm	24 inches	sprinkles	hundreds and thousands
1 kg	2 lb	77 cm	30 inches	thick cream	double/heavy cream

Published by Murdoch Books®, a division of Murdoch Magazines Pty Limited, 45 Jones Street, Ultimo NSW 2007.

Managing Editor: Jane Price **Designer:** Marylouise Brammer **Food Director:** Jody Vassallo **Food Editor:** Kathy Knudsen **Photographers:** Chris Jones, Reg Morrison (step photography) **Food Stylist:** Mary Harris **Food Preparation:** Kathy Knudsen, Kerrie Ray **Recipe Development:** Lulu Grimes, Kathy Knudsen, Michelle Lawton, Kerrie Ray, Lovoni Welch **Home Economists:** Rebecca Clancy, Michelle Lawton, Beth Mitchell, Kerrie Mullins, Justine Poole, Kerrie Ray **UK Consultant:** Maggi Altham **CEO & Publisher:** Anne Wilson **International Sales Director:** Mark Newman

National Library of Australia Cataloguing-in-Publication Data. Making Beautiful Cakes. Includes index. ISBN 0 86411 838 4. (Series: Family circle step-by-step). 641.8653
First printed 1998. Printed by Prestige Litho, Queensland. PRINTED IN AUSTRALIA.

The publisher thanks the following for help in the photography of this book: Chief Australia; Sunbeam Corporation Ltd; Kambrook; Sheldon & Hammond; Papaya Homewares; Ruby Star Traders; Limoges; The Bay Tree.

Index

almond icing, 6

berry cake, 75
boxes of gifts, 68
butter cake, 10
buttercream, 92
buttercream, coffee, 19, 55
buttercream, dark chocolate, 56
buttercream, milk chocolate, 39
buttercream, pink, 80
buttercream, white chocolate, 79, 84

candied citrus cake, 32
candied fruit, 64
candied rind, 32
cappuccino ice cream cake, 99
cappuccino truffle cake, 55
cappuccino truffles, 55
carrot cake, 12
chantilly cream, 87
cherry millefeuille, 47
chocolate buttercream, dark, 56
chocolate buttercream, milk, 39
chocolate buttercream, white, 79, 84
chocolate cake, 11
chocolate cake, sweet fig and, 92
chocolate collar, 48
chocolate curls, striped, 48
chocolate ganache, white, 36, 44, 48, 75, 83
chocolate glaze, 28, 72
chocolate glaze, dark, 67, 88
chocolate glaze, milk, 40
chocolate leaf cake, 67
chocolate mud cake, 14
chocolate waves, 40
Christening cake, 31
Christmas cake, 91
Christmas cakes, individual, 35
Christmas frosted fruits, 60
circles, toffee, 71
citrus cake, candied, 32
classic sponge, 17
coconut cake, 15
coconut custard cake, 104
coffee buttercream, 19, 55
collar cake, spotted, 19
collar, chocolate, 19, 48
collar, sponge, 87

continental wedding cake, 44
cornelli cake, two-tiered, 51
cream, chantilly, 87
cream cheese frosting, 20, 36, 71, 83
curls, striped chocolate, 48
custard, 104
custard cake, coconut, 104
custard filling, 44, 108
custard meringue gateau, 108

daisy cake, 107
daisy, pink lazy, 20
dark chocolate buttercream, 56
dark chocolate glaze, 67, 88

fig and chocolate cake, sweet, 92
floodwork flowers, 79
flowers, floodwork, 79
flowers, wedding, 96
frosted fruits, Christmas, 60
frosting, cream cheese, 20, 36, 71, 83
frosting, meringue, 51, 52, 75, 96, 104, 107
fruit box, ice cream, 23
fruit cake, 13
fruit cake, glacé-topped, 43
fruits, Christmas frosted, 60

ganache, white chocolate, 36, 44, 48, 75, 83
gateau, custard meringue, 108
gateau tiramisu, 24
genoise sponge, 16
gifts, boxes of, 68
glacé icing, 20
glacé-topped fruit cake, 43
glaze, 23
glaze, chocolate, 28, 72
glaze, dark chocolate, 67, 88
glaze, milk chocolate, 40
glazed cake, marble, 84
gold leaf cake, 88

halo, pears with a spun toffee, 59
hazelnut cake, toffee, 39

ice cream cake, cappuccino, 99
ice cream fruit box, 23
icing, 60
icing, almond, 6
icing, glacé, 20
icing, lemon, 32

icing, soft, 7
individual Christmas cakes, 35

leaf cake, chocolate, 67
lemon cream, 27
lemon curd, 100
lemon curd meringue cake, 100
lemon curd sponge, passionfruit and, 27
lemon icing, 32
lemon syrup, 100
lemons syrup cake, oranges and, 64

mango, striped cake with, 87
marble glazed cake, 84
marzipan *see* almond icing, 6
meringue cake, lemon curd, 100
meringue frosting, 51, 52, 75, 96, 104, 107
meringue gateau, custard, 108
meringue topping, 108
milk chocolate buttercream, 39
milk chocolate glaze, 40
millefeuille, cherry, 47
modelling paste, 7
mousse, 76
mousse cake, peach and orange, 76

orange mousse cake, peach and, 76
oranges and lemons syrup cake, 64

passionfruit and lemon curd sponge, 27
passionfruit topping, 27
peach and orange mousse cake, 76
pears with a spun toffee halo, 59
petal cake, rose, 52
pink buttercream, 80
pink lazy daisy, 20
presents, wrapped, 95

raspberry tuiles cake, 83
rose petal cake, 52
roses, sugared, 36

Saint Valentine's day, 80
soft icing, 7
sponge, classic, 17
sponge collar, 87

sponge, genoise, 16
sponge, passionfruit and lemon curd, 27
sponge with spun toffee, strawberries 'n' cream, 103
spotted collar cake, 19
star of the show, 72
stencil cake, 56
strawberries 'n' cream sponge with spun toffee, 103
striped cake with mango, 87
striped chocolate curls, 48
sugared roses, 36
sweet fig and chocolate cake, 92
syrup cake, oranges and lemons, 64

tiramisu, gateau, 24
toffee, 72
toffee circles, 71
toffee halo, pears with a spun, 59
toffee hazelnut cake, 39
toffee, strawberries 'n' cream sponge with spun, 103
topping, meringue, 108
topping, passionfruit, 27
traditional wedding cake, 63
triple truffle cake, 28
truffle cake, cappuccino, 55
truffle cake, triple, 28
truffles, 28, 72
truffles, cappuccino, 55
tuiles, 83
tuiles cake, raspberry, 83
twenty-first cake, star of the show, 72
two-tiered cornelli cake, 51

Valentine's day, Saint, 80

waves, chocolate, 40
wedding cake, continental, 44
wedding cake, traditional, 63
wedding flowers, 96
white chocolate buttercream, 79, 84
white chocolate ganache, 36, 44, 48, 75, 83
wrapped presents, 95